52 Biblical Principles
for Church Leaders

Leadership training for those who serve
within the environment of the church

Bishop Jesse Battle

LIVELY STONE
— PRESS —

52 Biblical Principles for Church Leaders

Published by Lively Stone Press
PO Box 623307
Oviedo, FL 32762

ISBN: 978-1-964081-40-3 paperback
Library of Congress Control Number 2024903842

Printed in the United States of America

10 9 8 7 6 5 4 3 2 1

Dedication

- *To the members, past and present, of the churches I've enjoyed the privilege of pastoring; their interactions with me made possible the writing of this instructional manual. To each of them, I am grateful.*

- *To the pastors whom I served as diocesan bishop, whose cooperation with my idiosyncratic leadership made possible the writing of this instructional manual. To them, I am grateful.*

- *To the pastors who, over the years, invited me to their pulpits to preach or teach. My observations of their varied ministry styles made possible the writing of this instructional manual. To each of them, I am grateful.*

- *To the bishops in whose dioceses I've preached or taught; my exposure to their leadership teams made possible the writing of this instructional manual. To each of them, I am grateful.*

- *To my siblings and in-laws whom I've pastored; their interactions with me made possible the writing of this instructional manual. To each of them, I am grateful.*

- *To my three children and eight grandchildren; my interactions with them made possible the writing of this instructional manual. To each of them, I am grateful.*

- *To my late wife, and my current wife of thirty-three years, Lady Denise Battle; our interactions made possible the writing of this instructional manual. To them, I am grateful.*

Contents

Contents

Foreword

By: Bishop Horace E. Smith, M.D.

"Another book on leadership… Do we need another?"

My desk, paper and electronic libraries, and portions of the floor of my home office, are strewn to overflowing with a myriad of tomes, from a diverse collection of authors, secular and spiritual, encompassing a wide range of areas of endeavors, stretching over hundreds of years of time. Some have been read thoroughly, countless numbers of times, until many of their pages have become dog-eared, and some simply perused in a cursory manner, their pages clean and almost untouched, pages stuck together because of lack of use.

Yet I have been reluctant to discard any of them. My wife would say that is because I am a bona fide hoarder, unwilling and almost unable to discard anything or anybody. I would characterize it a little differently, positing that I hold on to them because they speak to something primary in my spirit, and deeply engrained in my mind, that I believe impacts every area of life and living … Leadership!

Leadership—what a difficult and often hard-to-articulate concept. Many men and women of renown have tackled with great tenacity, the definition and subject of leadership. There are probably as many definitions of leadership as there are cultures and organizations. Defining it is often complicated and elusive. Allow me to share one that has helped me.

A tremendous churchman once shared his view about the critical nature of leadership as I sat in a national pastoral conference almost forty years ago as a young pastor. His words spoke deeply to my heart and helped shape my thinking and orientation regarding the place, and essentially, for quality leadership. I quote:

> *"The local church is the only hope of the world, and its future rests primarily in the hands of its leaders."*

The Church will flourish or falter largely on the basis of ***how we lead***.

God, in His unfathomable wisdom and incomprehensible judgment, has from the beginning of time, decided to use men and women, broken vessels, clay pots, to embrace, embody, and carry forward His divine purposes. God has decided that it is through called, prepared, anointed, and appointed leaders that His will and His work will be accomplished in the earth. This will be done as they, by faith, embrace truths and principles that emanate from the heart and mind of God.

Over the past several years, including those encompassing the recent biologic, economic, political, and sociological pandemics, it is my observation that tested principles and truths became the first casualties. Too often, principles have been almost discarded and replaced by individual constructs and dynamics of living, with pronouncements insisting on such phraseology as "my truth" and the "new reality." The acceptance and embracing of such concepts are presumptuous and flawed at best, and at worst challenge the singular sovereignty and authority of the Lord God. Such concepts and statements have even invaded the halls of trusted academic institutions of higher learning and sometimes the church itself. Truth too often replaced by popular opinions and "surveys"!

The Church of Jesus Christ is the lifeboat, the only rescue vehicle, that God has sent. Its primary responsibility is to announce, model, and present Christ to a dying world. God's love and grace is epitomized through the agency of godly leadership. Such leadership is called to utilize godly principles, to equip and empower Christians, who by the operation of the Holy Spirit will in turn impact souls, wherever they come in contact, all over the world, who by God's grace are birthed into His kingdom.

In his volume, *52 Biblical Principles for Church Leaders*, Bishop Jesse Battle has researched and compiled thoughts and sayings, distilled principles, and practices of leadership, that have been culled from the ranks of a wide cadre of leaders of the Church down through the years.

These principles, shared by men and women of faith, if correctly understood, embraced, and courageously applied, will become spiritual vehicles, used of God, to engender fresh faith, and a renewed confidence, that will transform and propel those who embrace them to new heights of glory in Christ Jesus.

In this day of uncertainty and chaos, I pray God gives each of us the spiritual insight and courage to embrace and incarnate genuine spiritual principles and truths in our daily lives.

—Bishop Horace E. Smith, M.D.

Introduction

52 *Biblical Principles for Church Leaders* is a book born out of a great passion for the church, and those whose lives are consumed by its mission. How that mission and the over-arching purpose of the church have been administered, during the time of my active service to the church, has been a source of concern for me during most of my senior adult life. Please, go with me on this journey of "instructional regret" as I explore what I witnessed over the past sixty years of the church's execution of the principles that either allowed the church to work seamlessly in pursuit of its mission, or, because of the mishandling of those principles, magnified the blunders that may have impeded the church's capacity to effectively administer its mission.

Very seldom does one get to do with his life only those things which he wishes to do. I can unequivocally say that, in retrospect, my life has wholly consisted of the things I wanted to do. While you might argue with me as to the veracity of that statement, remember, I am speaking in retrospect. That means after having the opportunity to look back over what I have done in life, I am at liberty to make such a statement. I admit, however, that I may not have felt that way twenty, thirty, forty, fifty years ago, while what I was doing was in the active stage. But now, now that the formative "doings of my life" are virtually over, I can say without equivocation, that what I have done is, for the most part, those things that I either wanted to do at the time I was doing them, or that I realize now that I should have wanted to do them.

Inclusive in those things is the fact that I have worked in almost every phase of leadership within the local church and beyond, from leadership within the district's youth department, to being appointed bishop over a multi-state diocese. I've enjoyed the blessed fortune of serving as a member of the board, or the board chair, of several civic organizations. My greatest "how to" learning curve was during my service in the corporate community, and with educational institutions. As I look back at the varied opportunities I have enjoyed, I still insist that I've done only those things that I wanted to do.

Mind you, they may not have been what I wanted to do at the time I was being "forced by life" to do them. But, having gone through them, having all the pieces together, having reached an age where I can look back over the grand scheme of things—they are *now* what I *wanted* to do! Do I have any regrets?

Yes, I've had regrets! Ironically, my biggest regret lies in the dubious way the church has executed its responsibilities to both its membership and the community at large. There seemed to have been, in some quarters of the church, an honest absence of any realization that functions of the church are guided by biblical principles that, when practiced, serve to demonstrate a noticeable level of godly uniformity in the way the church's activities are administered. My regrets are heightened by the reality that failure to operate at the required minimum basis in relationship to such biblical principles, places the church in an unwelcome status within the broader community. To me, it is most grievous when the church is viewed as *persona non grata* by those who could be tremendously helped by its mission of redemption.

It is my firm conviction, as is expressed in this manual, that when the church operates on the basis of sound biblical principles, it is far more beneficial to believers, and more attractive to non-believers. The advantage of initiating the transformation of non-believers into believers is chiefly that it is the biblically expressed mission of the church. Its challenge, as expressed in Titus 1:9 in reference to the duties of the bishop, is that all of us who serve the church as leaders *"may be able by sound doctrine both to exhort and to convince the gainsayers."*

If the church is to be acceptable and believable, its leaders must be trusted. If the leaders are to be trusted, they must operate based on indisputable biblical principles. The goal of this manual is to present those principles in a format that can be easily identified and adopted by those who serve in any leadership capacity within the church, or any organization, institution, or subsidiary of the church. Since a successful church can only be identified as such when it can be seen achieving the purpose for which it was created, it is incumbent upon those responsible for its well-being to understand the expectations placed upon them by those whom it serves.

I share these fifty-two lessons to that end. I do not now, nor will I ever, declare myself an expert in the leadership of the Lord's church. However, I am bound by the call of God placed upon my life to assist in the advancement of the kingdom of God to whatever degree God has prepared me to do so. The strategically placed experiences granted to us were not designed to merely enhance our image in life; but rather, they are designed for the benefit of the kingdom of God. After my voluntary retirement from the active ministry of pastoring a local church, I wrote a book titled, *God Is Not Finished with Me Yet.* God has and continues to invest far too much into my development for me to allow His investment to be buried in the sands of past service, and not sown into the ministry of those who are still actively engaged in effecting the image perceived by those who look upon the church. Whether such look be an act of skepticism, or in response to an earnest need for help, the integrity of the church must be upheld by those who serve as its gatekeepers.

I pray that this small contribution will go a long way in assisting those who are conscientiously pursuing the fulfillment of their responsibility to God by way of their leadership role in the Lord's sacred and beloved church.

—Bishop Jesse Battle

Principle 1

Church Leaders Must Be Chosen by God

For promotion cometh neither from the east, nor from the west, nor from the south. But God is the judge: He putteth down one, and setteth up another. —Psalm 75:6–7

Being appointed to a position of leadership in the church does not suggest that you are an expert in leadership, or the affairs of the church. Your being appointed does not imply that you are familiar with the plethora of nuances generally associated with the position to which you have been appointed. In most cases, your appointment simply suggests that either the person who appointed you saw in you the potential to do the job to which you were appointed, or that God inspired him to appoint you. In some instances, you may have been elected through the democratic process of being voted into such position. The appointment, or election, is the start of a long process of learning how to function in the responsibility to which you have been placed. At best, the start of your work as a church leader is an "on the job" learning experience.

While this holds true for almost any type of organization, and for any position or office into which a person may be placed, the church is unlike any other network of people in that it falls under the ultimate responsibility of God. As such, those selected to serve in leadership positions in the Lord's church should have, without exception, the sanction of God for such service. While such appointment into a leadership position may have been decided upon and announced by a higher-ranking person (i.e., department head, pastor, bishop), the inspiration for the appointment should have come from God. Even in cases where the leader may have been elected by popular vote, both the slate of candidates and the decision on which candidate one should vote for should come by the inspiration of God.

One can readily find a biblical precedent for this principle as the early church wrestled with the necessity to replace the position *"from which Judas by transgression fell,"* as is stated in Acts 1:25. Verse 24 reads: *"And they prayed, and said, Thou, Lord, which knowest the hearts of all men, shew whether of these two thou hast chosen."*

The ultimate choice of who serves in leadership in the church is the Lord's! Unfortunately, the irony is that, in today's church, for a large percentage of members and leaders, this would be regarded as folly. My response to that assertion starts with the Lord's Prayer. Verse 10 of the prayer in Matthew 6 says: *"Thy kingdom come. Thy will be done in earth, as it is in heaven."*

If the Lord's will is to be done in earth, it must begin with and in the Lord's church! God's will must then govern the appointment and election of church leaders at all levels of church administration. Without question, it must govern the pastorate! Where are the pastors who were chosen by God? It must govern the bishopric. Where are the bishops who were chosen by God? Conversely, God's will must govern all leadership personnel and functions of the church. Where are the superintendents, the auxiliary directors, the leaders of department, the local, district, national, and international officers who were chosen by God? These questions are not suggesting that such God-chosen leaders are not present. In the words of the Nashville country music artist, Austin Moody, in his country hit single, "I'm Just Saying…" Well, I'm just saying.

The degree to which the church allows the will of God to be exercised in its choices is directly related to the degree of spirituality by which the church is governed. It is, in fact, incumbent upon any church, or church organization, that wishes to be guided by the Spirit of God in its selection of leaders, to create an atmosphere in which the Holy Spirit can have free reign. This involves the development, by the leaders of such entity, of a close relationship with God. The closer such leaders become to God, the better they will come to know Him, and the easier it becomes for God to direct their decisions. This coincides with the biblical text that admonishes us to acknowledge the Lord in all our ways. The word *"acknowledge"* in this text means to *"come to know thoroughly"*—come to know God thoroughly in all your ways. While the text as rendered in the KJV is our primary reference, I am intrigued by the presentation of the New Living Translation. Please look at both translations of Proverbs 3:6:

> *In all thy ways acknowledge him, and he shall direct thy paths.* (KJV)

> *Seek his will in all you do, and he will show you which path to take.* (NLT)

Not only is it advantageous to a church to have God's direct involvement in its leadership choices—and, in fact, in all its choices—but it pleases God as well. After all, is not the church the bride of Christ? God is acutely concerned about the wellbeing of His church and its leaders. He makes this point in His discussion with the weeping prophet of Judah, whose lament was directly related to how Judah handled its affairs. We can imagine the prophets weeping today for God's church. God's declaration in Jeremiah 3:15 was (and is): *"...and I will give you pastors according to mine heart, which shall feed you with knowledge and understanding."*

The need for knowledge and understanding is still present! In fact, I suspect that it might be more needful today than it was in Jeremiah's days. As long as the leadership of the church demonstrates its alienation from the ways of God, the church operates in a state of imminent danger. As much as ever, the church's need for God-appointed leaders is still prevalent; and the need for the church's adherence to God's choices remains paramount.

Another indication of God's direct involvement in the leadership of His church is the psalmist's analysis of promotion. God alone is the judge; God promotes, and God demotes! *"For promotion cometh neither from the east, nor from the west, Nor from the south. But God is the judge: He putteth down one, and setteth up another"* (Psa. 75:6–7).

In conflict with the admonition stated above, there are those who have been placed in leadership positions in the church who were not sanctioned of God. It reminds me of Moses's rod in juxtaposition to the multiple rods of Pharoah's men! Clearly sanctioned by God, Moses threw down his rod and it became a serpent. Pharoah's magicians and soothsayers, sanctioned only by a godless king, threw down their rods. They, too, were transformed into serpents! As any leader who is sanctioned by God would expect, the single rod-turned-serpent of Moses, sanctioned by God, devoured the multiple rods-turned-serpents of Pharoah's servants. This was indeed the prophetic fulfillment of a New Testament text not yet written: *"Ye are of God, little children, and have overcome them: because greater is he that is in you, than he that is in the world"* (1 John 4:4).

Principle 1: Must Be Chosen by God

The ultimate success of church leaders at any level can only be achieved when such leaders are chosen by God! Please remember that the appearance of success is not success in Christ! Likewise, the trappings of success are not godly success! Know that sounding brass and tinkling cymbals do not an orchestra make.

Church leaders must be chosen by God!

The degree to which the church allows the will of God to be exercised in its choices is directly related to the degree of spirituality by which the church is governed.

Principle 2

Church Leaders Must Walk in Integrity

The integrity of the upright shall guide them: But the perverseness of transgressors shall destroy them.

—Proverbs 11:3

No responsible member of humanity would argue against the necessity of a solid commitment to the idea of integrity as a primary ingredient in their interactions with others. Dwight D. Eisenhower once said, "The supreme quality of leadership is integrity." One does not have to labor under the banner of Christianity to appreciate the value of integrity. It goes without saying that if any group of people is expected to demonstrate the principles of moral uprightness and honesty in their day-to-day business, it is those who represent Jesus Christ. It is the church!

Although it appears more necessary today than ever in the history of humanity, among Christians and non-Christians alike, there seems to be a tremendous short-coming in mankind's ability to handle the business of life in a manner that shows integrity. As the essential characteristic and custom of communities change, the urgency of Christian example becomes more and more important for Christian witness. The Bible emphatically calls the church *"the light of the world"* and *"the salt of the Earth."* The gospel makes it very clear that our light must not be hidden but must be placed upon a candlestick to give light to all that are around. We are reminded in the same text that salt which has lost its savor is henceforth good for nothing but to be trampled under the foot of men.

> *Ye are the salt of the earth: but if the salt have lost his savour, wherewith shall it be salted? it is thenceforth good for nothing, but to be cast out, and to be trodden under foot of men. Ye are the light of the world. A city that is set on an hill cannot be hid. Neither do men light a candle, and put it under a bushel, but on a candle- stick; and it giveth light unto all that are in the house. Let your light so shine before men, that they may see your good works, and glorify your Father which is in heaven.* (Matthew 5:13–16)

The question of opportunity has never been so conveniently posi- tioned as it is by the circumstances of today! A vast depreciation of the standards of moral behavior, which can be seen in every facet of life, creates a moral imperative that cannot, and must not, be ig- nored by the church. In his blatant attempt to minimize the church's impact on the community, Satan's destabilizing antics have unwit- tingly provided the church with an atmosphere in which even a modest degree of integrity would stand out as a bright light amid utter darkness. Apostle Paul commended the church in 2 Corin- thians 3:2–3, *"Ye are our epistle written in our hearts, known and read of all men: forasmuch as ye are manifestly declared to be the epistle of Christ ministered by us, written not with ink, but with the Spirit of the living God; not in tables of stone, but in fleshy tables of the heart."*

As crucial as it is that our interactions with those outside of our faith community be administered with the highest level of integrity, it is especially crucial for those who share the same church, the same jurisdiction, the same diocese, and/or the same denominational heritage—people with whom we interact on a regular or semi-regular basis during such events as councils, conferences, conventions, convocations, etc. To fail such clarion call is to fail the church and ultimately the God of the church. It is not uncommon for those who have been members of the same church for an extended period to develop strong personal relationships that allow them to disperse with the formalities required of casual acquaintances. At times, the interactions of longtime friends are so common that the niceties needed to preserve personal relationships are too often ignored. Close friendships are admirable, but they must never be allowed to erode the courtesies needed to support such friendships. The danger of such erosion is that minor disagreements can easily evolve into major conflict. I find it to be much more beneficial to retain such courtesies as "Thank you!" "Please!" "May I!" … than to mend the broken fences of perceived disrespect.

While the intent to disrespect may not be the aim of either party, if, however, either party feels disrespected, resultant hostility has been planted. At that point, I strongly suggest that both parties go immediately into "relationship salvage" mode. That requires leaders to do what some intuitively find difficult, to set aside their pride and egotistical posturing, and take on a genuine spirit of humility. Such humility can be difficult because it goes against the grain of character traits often inherent to successful leaders. Albeit, when we find ourselves in positions where the absence of courtesy has caused strife, we must deal with the strife before it festers into something far more dangerous than a mere misunderstanding. The writer of Proverbs recommends a soft answer for those who find themselves in this position. He wrote in Proverbs 15:1, *"A soft answer turneth away wrath: But grievous words stir up anger."*

A leader could simply choose to do nothing, but that would demonstrate a gross lack of integrity. I see too many church leaders simply walk away as if they're not responsible for what transpired because of their lack of "interactional protocol," the common rules and courtesies that normally govern our interactions with others—superiors, equals, or subordinates. This includes casual acquaintances, close friends, and those in between or beyond. The reality is that "inter-church conflict" can be averted if friends practice the principle of integrity in dealing with each other, and not take the relationship for granted. The principle of integrity mandates that those serving in leadership positions within the church—local, regional, or national—do everything within their power to ensure the integration of mutual respect in all interactions, and that the goal of fostering the peaceful coexistence of all members and guests remain at the forefront of all communications and activities. And, of course, this task requires absolute honesty of intent and presentation in all such interactions.

Church leaders must walk in integrity!

Principle 3

Church Leaders Must Be Willing to Follow Leadership

Yea, all of you be subject one to another, and be clothed with humility. ...   —1 Peter 5:5

Remembered in the legacy of the late Sam Rayburn, is a rousing speech made to fellow congressional colleagues in which he admonished them to be good leaders while, at the same time, being good followers. Rayburn, a twenty-four-term congressman, and the longest-serving speaker of the United States House of Representatives, argued, "You cannot be a leader, and ask other people to follow you, unless you know how to follow, too." This is not some magical function that applies only to Congress. Quite the contrary, this applies to any endeavor where a person is designated to lead other people. This principle of leadership has been evident in the New Testament church since its inception. Simply put, every leader must be a follower, because every leader has a leader! The degree to which we are good leaders is directly proportional to our ability to be good followers. While every follower may not possess the characteristics of a leader, any leader who does not demonstrate the ability to follow effectively, will be a dysfunctional leader at best.

The ability to be an effective follower is not only necessary *after* a person becomes a leader, but it also begins long before the option of leadership becomes available. If potential leaders are ever going to become great leaders, leadership training must begin during their developmental years as followers.

Young adolescents who will not follow the directions of parents or older siblings do injury to later attempts to lead. Teenagers who will not follow the instructions of teachers and coaches forfeit their chances of success as leaders. Young adults who refuse to listen to the admonitions of older adults sacrifice their potential to lead. Middle-aged persons who are disdainful of the advice of elders cannot effectively lead the young or middle-aged. Finally, seniors who have never been manageable will never be able to manage others. Every leader must be a follower, because every leader has a leader!

While it is true that God is the ultimate leader in the affairs of the church, it is equally true that God works through the agency of humanity. As such, the intermediate leadership that operates from human to human is another human. Just as ushers must follow the lead or head usher who, in turn, follows the director, the director must follow the guidelines of the pastor, or the person designated by the pastor to direct the ushering activities of the church. I have encountered ushers whose claim was, "I follow God!" The irony is that their ushering tenure was short-lived because they refused to follow their leader. This scenario can apply to any other auxiliary within the local church, including the ministerial board. While the hierarchy of church leadership ultimately stops at God, it is supported by "human aid stations" along the way. Again, every leader must be a follower, because every leader has a leader!

As you advance in your service to the church, you may someday be called upon to serve as senior pastor of a local church. This change in service does not remove you from the "leader-follower/ follower-leader" responsibilities in the "God-humanity/humanity-God" hierarchy of inter-church leadership. Pastors must contend with multiple levels that provide some element of oversight of their leadership activities. Church boards, civic agencies, governmental entities must all be reckoned with in the performance of pastoral duties. In addition, there may be multiple levels of denominational leaders. Depending on the protocols of the reformation, there will likely be conference and/or diocese leaders to whom pastors may be accountable to varying degrees. The next level of human leadership is the broader organizational leaders and boards to which pastors and bishops may be responsible. And, as if that is not enough, there are lawyers, legal entities, the IRS, etc., all providing leadership for the leaders! Again, every leader must be a follower, because every leader has a leader!

It is important to note that being a follower does not negate your capacity to lead! However, as has been pointed out, failure to be a follower does indeed negate the capacity to lead. In the "fraternity of leaders," there seems to be an attitude that suggests that anything that can be perceived as an infringement upon leadership, compromises the leader's sovereignty as a leader. I apologize for not having made this point clear, but there is no inherent sovereignty, apart from God, in church leadership. The church leader is not a king or a dictator; rather, he is a servant to those who follow!

Jesus responded to the question raised by His disciples of which of them would be the greatest. He made it crystal clear that the greatest among you is he who is willing to serve. Greatness must be defined by both ability and willingness to serve. Great leaders must not only know how to serve their constituents, but they must also be willing to serve. Willingness to serve requires a leader to come down from the lofty pinnacle of leadership to the valley of daily service. It is in that valley that all good leaders must ultimately reside. Robert Greenleaf, a noted author who founded the "modern servant leadership movement," acknowledged: "The first and most important choice a leader makes is the choice to serve, without which the capacity to lead is severely limited." Simon Sinek, a nationally known author and inspirational speaker, concurred by noting: "Leadership is not about being in charge. Leadership is about taking care of those in your charge."

The proving ground to the call into greater service is the capacity to serve faithfully in lesser service. The person who cannot faithfully lead an auxiliary of six is bound to encounter serious trouble trying to lead a congregation of six thousand. Jesus said, in Luke 16:10, *"He that is faithful in that which is least is faithful also in much: and he that is unjust in the least is unjust also in much."*

Church leaders must be willing to follow leadership!

Principle 4

Church Leaders Must Respect Subordinates

And above all things have fervent charity among your-
selves: for charity shall cover the multitude of sins. Use
hospitality one to another without grudging. As every man
hath received the gift, even so minister the same one to
another, as good stewards of the manifold grace of God.
                                                    —1 Peter 4:8–10

I do not like our use of the word "subordinates" in reference to members of the Lord's church! I have a great disdain for the implications suggested by its general misuse. I especially reject the elitist attitude often evident in the expressions of those who find comfort in talking about their "subordinates." They often speak as if referring to an "underclass" who could never be on their level. The definition of the word "subordinate," when used as a noun, refers to a person under the authority of another within an organizational structure. The problem is that too many of our actions operate from the verb definition, which is to regard someone as of lesser importance.

We may not need to travel far into the world to experience this negative treatment. Just look around your church, its ministries, and auxiliaries; you may very well find yourself smack in the middle of such demeaning disrespect and disregard, right in the church!

"Subordination anxiety" is the unnecessary frustration that we often put our brothers and sisters through when we treat them as if they are "nobodies" next to us. Not only is this behavior a sin, but its psychological effects on those treated as lower, inferior, or minor persons almost parallel what the Bible categorized as abominations. Many good members are driven from the church by members and leaders alike who operate in this false sense of superiority. It's no wonder that we are cautioned in Scripture not to think more highly of ourselves: *"For I say, through the grace given unto me, to every man that is among you, not to think of himself more highly than he ought to think; but to think soberly, according as God hath dealt to every man the measure of faith"* (Rom. 12:3).

To be effective leaders, we must learn to respect those who follow our leadership. This inclusionary level of respect is required, if for no other reason than because we are leading God's heritage. Apostle Peter warned the elders that they are not *"lords over God's heritage"* (1 Pet. 5:3).

A few years ago, I saw a window sticker on the back of a family van that carried the message, "Caution, precious cargo aboard." That driver obviously respected and valued the passengers whom I presumed were his or her children. I mention this because church leaders must write a similar message upon the windows of their hearts.

Godly leaders are acutely aware that those who follow their leadership must not be bullied into compliance; they must not be verbally or psychologically beaten into cooperating with their leadership. General Dwight Eisenhower, a four-star general of the Army, who later became president of the United States, said during the ceremony of his promotion to one of only five, five-star generals of the Army, "You don't lead by hitting people over the head—that's assault, not leadership!" Church leaders are not called to assault the people of God; rather, as Apostle Peter declared, to *"feed the flock of God which is among you, taking the oversight thereof, not by constraint, but willingly; not for filthy lucre, but of a ready mind"* (1 Pet. 5:2).

Newly appointed church leaders, along with some veteran leaders, must remember that respect as leaders is not deserved until it is first earned. Once placed into a position of leadership, leaders are faced with the realization that there may exist a different dichotomy as a leader versus that experienced as a lay-member in the same church. In some instances, the change may be brought about, or at least, aided, by the subtle change in personality detected in newly appointed leaders. However, in other cases, the personality may have pretty much remained intact while members react differently wholly because of the new leadership role.

For years, I wrestled with the idea of trying to identify the cause of the shift in attitudes of both those who are led and newly appointed leaders. Other than the comments shared above, I can only conclude that the human personality is often variable and unpredictable. Unable to document any justifying rationale, I adopted the philosophy of Dr. Alfred Adler, an Austrian medical doctor and psychotherapist, who became internationally known for his work in individual psychology. Adler's emphasis on the importance of one's feelings made him a leader in the area of psychotherapy. His conclusion that the only explanation a person needs to justify his actions is that he is human, set an explosive tone in the area of individual psychology.

Some attitudes encountered by newly appointed or elected church leaders, as they connect with those for whom they are responsible, will follow an identifiable path of logical thinking; however, leaders may also encounter other attitudes that will leave them utterly bewildered. In either case, leaders must exhibit the same level of respect and care for individual members in both groups. The leader's job is not to analyze or categorize followers; rather, it is to lead them in the areas of assigned responsibilities. In an effort to encourage confused and discouraged church leaders, allow me to remind you that you do have access to the God who called you into the leadership service of His church!

Access to God is twofold: it can be a meaningful resource making a difference between fear and confidence; it also creates an irrevocable responsibility by which leaders are ultimately judged. Because of that resource, leaders are without excuse if they behave otherwise. God holds leaders accountable for how we treat followers. Jesus talked about that responsibility in Matthew 25:40. He said during a private conversation with His disciples, *"Verily I say unto you, Inasmuch as ye have done it unto one of the least of these my brethren, ye have done it unto me."*

Church leaders must respect subordinates!

Principle 5

Church Leaders Must Exercise Self-Discipline

...but I discipline my body and make it my slave, so that, after I have preached to others, I myself will not be disqualified.
—1 Corinthians 9:27 (NASB)

For the purpose of this discussion, I would like to emphasize three aspects of self-discipline that are especially important for those who desire to serve as leaders in the Lord's church.

1. Self-discipline is regarded as the ability to overcome one's impulses, and to regulate one's behavior, thoughts, and emotions.

2. Self-discipline is generally reflected in one's ability to control his feelings and overcome his weaknesses.

3. Self-discipline is the ability to pursue what is right, especially in the face of contrary influences.

Many psychologists agree that much of what members of the human race do on a daily basis is the result of the multiple impulses that average people wrestle with during the course of life. These impulses, formed over a period of many years, influence emotions, thoughts, and ultimately, behavior. The formation of these impulses can be traced back to a child's formative years, resulting from how the child is raised, and how he interprets the perceptions of others towards him. Being raised in a strong Catholic city, I recall hearing slogans that inundated our community regarding the enrollment of children in Catholic schools. I cannot recall the verbatim wording of the slogans, but I remember one suggestion that by letting Catholic schools have the child during his formative years, he would be a Catholic for life. The rationale was that impulses formed during his early years would influence him throughout life.

Other contributing influences might include the influence of peers and peer groups upon a child. Peers and peer groups can be defined as any person or group with whom a child has consistent interactions. This could include neighborhoods, schools, churches, workplaces, social organizations, and any other entity that touches the child's life on a regular basis. Parents and church leaders who are cognizant of the impact of the influences of such peer groups are more sensitive to the types of environments within which their children are socialized. This speaks to the efficacy of the admonition of Proverbs 22:6: *"Train up a child in the way he should go: And when he is old, he will not depart from it."*

The urgent need to develop in its constituency the ability to control feelings and overcome weaknesses is not exclusive to church leaders. All people, no matter their affiliation or lack of affiliation with the church, must exercise some level of control over the reactions caused by their feelings and weaknesses. Because of the broad spectrum of influence held by some church leaders, the negative impact upon a church, or larger community, may be more acute than that caused by a non-leader's lack of self-control. The ability to manage oneself is so imperative that failure to do so could cause a tremendous ripple effect within the church, or any auxiliary of the church. I have seen entire congregations destroyed when the lack of control was evident in a senior pastor. A lack of self-discipline can be one of the most urgent dangers to the survival of the church, or auxiliary. For this reason, church leaders must prayerfully and studiously seek God's help for the management of such grave deficiencies. A conscientious church leader, whose heart is for those whom he has been assigned to lead, will do what is necessary to exercise, and demonstrate, a sufficient level of self-discipline.

The lack of self-control can be marginal to the extent that it is hardly visible in the daily activities of some leaders. On the other hand, it can be so out of control that it literally interferes with the leader's ability to successfully conduct day-to-day responsibilities. Then, there are those extreme cases where lack of self-control reaches such a disturbing level that it almost seems demonic. I have seen cases where many of the symptoms of demonic possession are evident. There is a glaring case study in the New Testament of a man who was possessed with demons. When carefully analyzed, his actions could provide a clue to the type of behavior that is consistent with such demonic possession. I am not suggesting that all demon-possessed people behave in an identical pattern as this man; neither am I suggesting that people who display or mimic some of the behavioral patterns of this man are demon possessed. Whatever our conclusions might be of this man, or others whose similarly alarming behavior they may have witnessed, let us take a cursory look at the narrative in Matthew 8:28–29:

> *And when he was come to the other side into the country of the Gergesenes, there met him two possessed with devils, coming out of the tombs, exceeding fierce, so that no man might pass by that way. And, behold, they cried out, saying, What have we to do with thee, Jesus, thou Son of God? art thou come hither to torment us before the time?*

While in the synoptic gospels, the narratives are generally repre-
sentative of the same event, they are accounted for through the eyes
of each writer as he looks through the prism of his own culture.
Because of that factor, I would like to consider the presentation of
both Mark and Luke, as well as that of Matthew. I would love to
share the metaphorical exegesis of each occurrence in each narrative to extrapolate the similarities between how the subject in the
text behaved versus how a demon-possessed person of this gener-
ation might behave. However, this manuscript does not lend itself
to that lengthy analysis. Nonetheless, the narratives of Mark and
Luke are as follows:

> *And when [Jesus] was come out of the ship, immediate-*
> *ly there met him out of the tombs a man with an unclean*
> *spirit, who had his dwelling among the tombs; and no*
> *man could bind him, no, not with chains: because that*
> *he had been often bound with fetters and chains, and the*
> *chains had been plucked asunder by him, and the fetters*
> *broken in pieces: neither could any man tame him. And*
> *always, night and day, he was in the mountains, and*
> *in the tombs, crying, and cutting himself with stones.*
> *But when he saw Jesus afar off, he ran and worshipped*
> *him, and cried with a loud voice, and said, What have I*
> *to do with thee, Jesus, thou Son of the most high God?*
> *I adjure thee by God, that thou torment me not.* (Mark
> 5:2–7)

> *And when he went forth to land, there met him out of*
> *the city a certain man, which had devils long time, and*
> *ware no clothes, neither abode in any house, but in the*
> *tombs. When he saw Jesus, he cried out, and fell down*
> *before him, and with a loud voice said, What have I to*
> *do with thee, Jesus, thou Son of God most high? I be-*
> *seech thee, torment me not. (For he had commanded the*

unclean spirit to come out of the man. For oftentimes it had caught him: and he was kept bound with chains and in fetters; and he brake the bands, and was driven of the devil into the wilderness.) And Jesus asked him, saying, What is thy name? And he said, Legion: because many devils were entered into him. (Luke 8:27–30)

The necessity of self-discipline is such a required principle for church leaders that I would be remiss if I did not share the conclusion of the above-mentioned narratives in which each writer found it expedient to point out that once the demons were cast out, he followed the purpose of Jesus. A church leader who wrestles with the capacity (or lack of) to exercise and maintain a sufficient level of self-discipline can remedy the problem by following the guidance and leading of the Holy Spirit. Another source of assistance is the advice and counseling of a senior leader. As a church leader, I advise you to prayerfully consult with God for deliverance until He speaks to your spirit as He did to Paul: *"My grace is sufficient for thee: for my strength is made perfect in weakness"* (2 Cor. 12:9).

Church leaders must exercise self-discipline!

A conscientious church leader, whose heart is for those whom he has been assigned to lead, will do what is necessary to exercise, and demonstrate, a sufficient level of self-discipline.

Principle 6

Church Leaders Must Operate in Fairness

*Blessed are they who observe justice, who do righteous-
ness at all times!* —Psalm 106:3 (ESV)

*For ye are all the children of God by faith in Christ Jesus.
For as many of you as have been baptized into Christ
have put on Christ ... for ye are all one in Christ Jesus.*
—Galatians 3:26–28

Having served as a leader in the church for more than half a
century—starting during my late teen years as vice president of the district youth department and, for a brief period, as president prior to my twentieth birthday, and also having
been appointed by the bishop of the diocese to my first pastorate at
the age of twenty—I have served in multiple leadership positions
in the church. In addition, having served in leadership roles in vocational institutions, academia, and later in several civic organizations, I have lived in, or very close to, leadership. I understand the
role of leadership in the church and outside of the church. One of
the greatest leadership mistakes I have consistently witnessed, both
in the church and the broader community, is the lack of fairness in
how the general constituency is treated. There seems to exist within
leadership, a gross misunderstanding of what fairness looks like.

While such behavior outside the church might be tolerable, unfairness must never become part of the administration of the church. Unfairness is exhibited by repeated displays of partiality in such areas as economic conditions, gender, and race, to name a few. If there exists any institution on earth where impartiality should be the mainstay, it is the church. The church must not yield to the political or social pressure of partiality. No matter what factors are used to justify acts of partiality, they must never infiltrate the sanctity of the church! Apostle Paul emphasized this point in discussions with the church at Rome: *"There is no respect of persons with God"* (Rom. 2:11). The English Standard Version (ESV) puts it bluntly: *"For God shows no partiality."*

My early leadership years taught me what I consider to be the most valuable lesson any leader could learn. That lesson established the model for my future leadership experiences. I have practiced and taught it during leadership seminars throughout the country. That rule is that all members within a common group must be treated the same! Given the same circumstances, what a leader is willing to do for one person in the group, he must be willing to do for all members of the group. Of course, there may arise, from time to time, extraneous circumstances unique to one person in certain situations. But, when presented with the same factors, the leader must be willing to provide the same assistance to any member. At no point should a member be singled out and treated with favors that are not available to other members. Please note, there may be instances where members of a particular class within a group may be treated in a way that members outside of that class are not treated. Still, in the instance of "class-based" differentiation, all members of that class must be treated the same. An example of class differentiation may be that the administrative team of a group may be treated to a special outing in appreciation for the long hours they spend in planning the activities of the group. Even though the entire membership is not treated to the event, it must be offered to *all* administrative team members. The appearance of partiality must be avoided!

In the gospel of James, we find a strong narrative against partiality in the church. James writes:

> *My brothers, show no partiality as you hold the faith in our Lord Jesus Christ, the Lord of glory. For if a man wearing a gold ring and fine clothing comes into your assembly, and a poor man in shabby clothing also comes in, and if you pay attention to the one who wears the fine clothing and say, "You sit here in a good place," while you say to the poor man, "You stand over there," or, "Sit down at my feet," have you not then made distinctions among yourselves and become judges with evil thoughts?* (James 2:1–4 ESV)

There is much talk in both the Old and New Testaments about justice, which, in traditional terms, means giving one what is due. The word itself makes no reference to whether what is due is good or bad; that depiction is determined by the deeds that precipitated it. It does, however, regard fairness to the degree that each person gets what is rightfully deserved. The overarching idea of justice is that it deals in fairness. In ancient times, it was considered fair to give someone in return what he meted out. If good was given, then good is to be returned; if, however, evil was given, then evil is returned. While not synonyms, the two words, "justice" and "fairness," have a symbiotic relationship. Justice denotes the philosophical (and ethical) suggestion that all people are to be treated impartially. The Bible is replete with calls for justice! What moves justice into the realm of Christianity is that it is often tempered by mercy, which, when requested and applied, softens the response rightfully due as the result of wrong deeds. While the church, and church leaders, must administer justice, and must do so impartially, such justice must be served with mercy. If not, the church ceases to be the church of the Lord.

"Blessed are they who observe justice, who do righteousness at all times!" (Psa. 106:3 ESV). Like justice, another word that runs throughout biblical text is "righteousness"! While righteousness denotes being in right standing with God, such right standing is intricately connected to, and cannot be achieved apart from, an active commitment to justice. An astute Bible student will readily recognize the link between one's standing with God and his relationship with, and treatment of, fellow believers. A case in point lies in the connection between God's forgiveness of us, and our forgiveness of others. Jesus's instructions on prayer emphasize such a link. Jesus instructed His disciples that when they pray, they should say, *"And forgive us our debts, as we forgive our debtors"* (Matt. 6:12). The Luke 11:4 rendition is the same: *"And forgive us our sins; for we also forgive everyone that is indebted to us."* Paul furthered this point with the church at Colossae: *"Forbearing one another, and forgiving one another, if any man have a quarrel against any: even as Christ forgave you, so also do ye"* (Col. 3:13).

Another indication of the *"us/others-God/us"* relationship of righteousness can be found in the admonition given to those who bring their gift to God while in ought with their brother: *"Therefore if thou bring thy gift to the altar, and there rememberest that thy brother hath ought against thee; leave there thy gift before the altar, and go thy way; first be reconciled to thy brother, and then come and offer thy gift"* (Matt. 5:23–24).

This lesson will not afford me the opportunity to exhaust the biblical indication of the relationship between our capacity for justice as demonstrated by our willingness to be impartial, and our righteousness before God. I conclude this lesson by affirming such relationship by way of the admonition given by Jesus in Matthew 25:40,

45: *"Verily I say unto you, Inasmuch as ye have done it unto one of the least of these my brethren, ye have done it unto me…. Then shall he answer them, saying, Verily I say unto you, Inasmuch as ye did it not to one of the least of these, ye did it not to me."* Psalm 106:3 (ESV) confirms that those *"who observe justice"* are those *"who do righteousness"*! He said, *"Blessed are they who observe justice, who do righteousness at all times!"*

Church leaders must *do* righteousness; otherwise, they are not ethically, morally, or spiritually prepared to serve in the leadership of the Lord's church. Paradoxically, the leader's observation of impartiality and justice is imperative in the exercise of such righteousness. Any church leader who fails to operate in such manner will never rise to the level of the challenge required by God of church leaders.

Church leaders must operate in fairness!

Church leaders must do righteousness; otherwise, they are not ethically, morally, or spiritually prepared to serve in the leadership of the Lord's church.

Principle 7

Church Leaders Must Exercise Patience

Therefore, as God's chosen people, holy and dearly loved, clothe yourselves with compassion, kindness, humility, gentleness and patience. —Colossians 3:12 (NIV)

As difficult as it is, I must refrain from labeling any of the "52 Biblical Principles for Church Leaders" as being the most important, because, in reality, they are all "most" important. I mention this now because, unquestionably, patience ranks at the top of the list in terms of paramount necessity for a successful experience in any endeavor in life. I have witnessed the devastation of major projects—devastation that could only be attributed to a lack of patience. I have seen the destruction of previously performed good works destroyed because of a single rant of impatience. There is a Chinese proverb which states, "One moment of patience may ward off great disaster. On the other hand, one moment of impatience may ruin a whole life." Ironically, one of the immediate results of impatience is frustration, which often leads to uncontrolled anger. For others, impatience can result in a type of temper tantrum, which places one into a most tenable position in the eyes of those witnessing from the outside.

While impatience cannot be wholly attributed to immaturity, there is definitely a relationship between immaturity and impatience!

Parents of newborn babies often experience the frustration of impatience in their reaction to the infant who wants to be fed, and fed now! This cannot be classified as learned behavior since we are often talking about infants who are but days old. The unbridled screaming, the frantic waving of the arms, and the kicking of the legs are natural behaviors in response to the infant not immediately getting what he wants. A new mother often drops whatever she is doing and rushes to accommodate the wishes of the baby. While feeding the baby is absolutely appropriate, doing so in the process of the tantrum certifies the appropriateness of the tantrum in the psyche of the infant. In his developing brain, the tantrum is what brought about the feeding. To the baby, this establishes the pattern for how he should act when he cannot have his way in the future.

The development of the harmful effects of impatience can be easily prevented by establishing, and sticking with, a feeding schedule. The schedule will, among other things, eliminate the formation of the tantrum-based feeding cycle in the mind of the infant. As he matures, his relationship with other wants and needs will be modeled, in part, from his feeding experience. Adolescent psychologists agree that the patterns formulated during infancy often aid in shaping behavior that will be displayed during the lifetime of the person. Felix Ravaisson, considered to be France's most influential philosopher during the second half of the nineteenth century, published *Of Habit*, which is still regarded as a major work on the formation of habits[1]. His contention was: "Actions that are repeated over time gradually become habits, with a curious life of their own." He was an avid exponent of the idea that habits develop unconsciously, from internal and external stress.

Obviously, the antidote to the formation of negative habits is patience! In the above referenced text (Colossians 3:12 NIV), Paul

---

1   Ravaisson, F., (1838). *Of Habit*. Kessinger Publishing

reminds the saints that they are God's chosen people, holy and dearly loved. He admonishes them to clothe themselves with five synonymous character traits. Even though the list varies slightly among translations, I chose the NIV translation because of the close association of the nuance of each word to the characteristics of patience. He wrote, *"Therefore, as God's chosen people, holy and dearly loved, clothe yourselves with compassion, kindness, humility, gentleness and patience."*

This text applies to all persons laboring under the banner of Christianity, but I find it particularly critical for those who function as church leaders. Leaders in the church work with the yoke of an even higher calling. The absence of patience in the execution of the leader's day-to-day responsibilities must never become the pattern of those called upon to lead any segment of the church. Not only must an abundance of patience be evident, but it must also be seen as the hallmark of all leadership activities. When church members fail to display patience in their response to such leadership, the leader must exemplify patience as the standard modus operandi. Jesus said it best in Luke 12:42: *"For unto whomsoever much is given, of him shall be much required: and to whom men have committed much, of him they will ask the more."*

Patience can be defined as one's ability to tolerate the unexpected without becoming angry, or out of balance. Patience can be further defined as the capacity to continue on course, despite the advent of unanticipated difficulties. Having patience means to have the strength to suffer without being annoyed by the cause of the suffering, or to complain about the suffering. Among the visible evidence of patience is the manifestation of calmness despite the propensity for trouble caused by the impending disruption. I remember reading a quote (I don't recall by whom) that suggested that patience is not just the ability to wait, but it is the ability to keep a good attitude while waiting. Like most good things in life, patience is not easy to acquire or maintain. It must be continuously cultivated through the process of hard work and faithful reliance on God.

I encourage newly appointed or elected church leaders to commit themselves to an active regimen of prayer and meditation wherein the primary objective is the acquisition of patience for their impending task of leadership. Allow the Holy Spirit to minister to you on a regular basis, as you confront the challenge of leading the people of God with calmness of spirit and confidence of heart; for these two attributes form the groundwork of the development of the kind of patience upon which you can build a successful leadership experience.

Church leaders must exercise patience!

Principle 8

Church Leaders Must Be Students of the Bible

Study to shew thyself approved unto God, a workman that needeth not to be ashamed, rightly dividing the word of truth. —2 Timothy 2:15

Inasmuch as the patterns and practices of the Christian church are wholly based in Scripture, one who wishes to become conversant in its practices must acquaint himself with the various narratives contained in Scripture. The more knowledgeable of such patterns one becomes, the more conversant he will become in the application of Scripture. Since none of us were here during the formation of the church, we must rely on the historical record found in the Holy Writ. Of course, as any serious Bible scholar can attest, the formation of the church did not begin with the New Testament. Quite the contrary, if we are to truly understand the mind of God in the creation of His church, our journey of biblical exploration must start at the start of the Bible. The first verse of the first chapter of the first book of the Bible sets the premise for the existence of the Bible and the church. Subsequently, every verse of every chapter of every book thereafter builds upon the unfolding theology of Genesis 1:1: *"In the beginning God created the heaven and the earth."* This text declares the preeminence of God and the sovereignty of God to the point that everything else about God is based upon His authority of such performance, and His right in doing so. The fact that God was in the beginning demonstrates His superiority over all persons and things in and of the heavens and the earth; it makes God first in all things.

> *For by him were all things created, that are in heaven, and that are in earth, visible and invisible, whether they be thrones, or dominions, or principalities, or powers: all things were created by him, and for him: and he is before all things, and by him all things consist.* (Colossians 1:16–17)

In like manner, as God was in the beginning with no one or anything else, He shares neither time nor space with any entity outside of Himself. His right, or supreme authority, cannot be challenged. The divine sovereignty of God is without question! As a matter of record, I must point out that even though the creative process is full blown, God's divine sovereignty remains unquestionable. As such, we must all accept the authority of God's Word as the accurate record of the essence of God. We must give full credence to all its narratives, its authority, and its totally absolute infallibility. We accept God's Word as His revelation of what He has done, what He is doing, and what He shall do!

For the maintenance of the Lord's church, it is imperative that every church leader fully embrace the authenticity of the Word of God as the exact revelation of God, His creative works, His salvational plan, and its full implementation. The work of the Lord's church must be guided by biblical truth! However, biblical truth can never be ascertained by our familiarization with, or the absorption of, a few favorite Scriptures! Truth comes as the result of an overall familiarity with the entire context of Scripture. While this is not accomplished overnight, the challenge of understanding the overall context of the Bible is ever unfolding through the process of consistent interaction with Scripture. We must not wait until we are appointed, or elected, to a leadership position to begin such process; the delicate task of reading, hearing, and understanding biblical truth must be as much a part of a new Christian's diet as breastmilk is to a newly born infant. The commitment of church leaders to facilitate such feedings must be as passionately done as that of a mother towards her child.

During the early days of my military experience, I learned an acronym that has stuck with me since that time. It left an impression so indelible that I look for it in organizations of all types, religious or otherwise. The acronym, "SOP," stands for "Standard Operating Procedures." Every unit I became a part of, from the Army Induction Center to the Army Helicopter Flight School, had its own SOP! This was a manual containing detailed instructions on every aspect of the duties and procedures pertaining to that unit. All duties and responsibilities required of any Army officer assigned to the unit were addressed in the SOP! The unfortunate thing was that there were soldiers, both enlisted men and officers, who failed to familiarize themselves with the SOP. The problem caused by such failure was when the soldier failed to perform an assignment adequately, he was without excuse. All the necessary instructions were in the SOP!

For the church, the Bible is the primary SOP! It contains all standard operating procedures of the church. No stone is left unturned; no question is left unanswered for how the church, its leaders, or its members are to act in given situations. Like men in my Army units, some leaders fail to familiarize themselves with the Bible. The result of their knowledge deficiency about procedures and protocol, patterns and practices, disputes and resolutions, sin and righteousness, the doctrine of God and the doctrines of devils, about all aspects of the church, is that it has been severely crippled in its ability to accomplish its God-given mission.

If the church is to find its way in this jungle of religiosity where ecumenicity has become the common practice, and there is no distinction between denominational doctrine, it must raise up a cadre of leaders who are committed to its foundational principles. There must be an exodus from the free-fall religious practices of today, back to sound biblical teaching lifted directly and intact from the narratives of the Bible. Church leaders at all levels must enroll again into the school of sound biblical practice. The Bible must return to its God-intended position as the anchor for the church as it navigates the torrential seas of life. For to do otherwise would inflict great pain upon the righteous, and that is far too great a price to pay. The urgent question raised by the psalmist, which can still be heard in its cries to the leaders of the twenty-first-century church, is: *"If the foundations be destroyed, What can the righteous do?"* (Psa. 11:3).

In order to reclaim the purpose for which God created the church, and to save the remnant of the church...

...church leaders must be students of the Bible!

Principle *9*

Church Leaders Must Be Willing to Make Personal Sacrifices

This is how we know love: Jesus laid down his life for us, and we ought to lay down our lives for our brothers and sisters. But if someone has material possessions and sees a brother or sister in need but refuses to help—how can the love of God dwell in a person like that? Little children, let's not love with words or speech but with action and truth. This is how we will know that we belong to the truth. —1 John 3:16–19 (CEB)

Throughout the Bible, great spiritual leaders have been known for their selfless deeds on behalf of other people. Moses risked his life because he was called to deliver God's people out of the oppressions of Egypt. Abraham gave up everything he had because he was directed by God to go into a strange land so that God could establish a new nation through him. The prophets, both major and minor, were known for their life-risking sacrifices for the cause of their calling. Esther could have died had not the king extended his scepter to welcome her into his presence. The disciples of Jesus Christ, ordinary men in many ways, were subjected to the possibility of the same fate that awaited Jesus at the hands of the Roman soldiers.

Without a Saul-turned-Paul on a Damascus Road, there would not be a first or second epistle to the church at Corinth. The inspiring words of 1 Corinthians 1:1–2 would not echo in the hearts of church leaders throughout the world: *"Paul, called to be an apostle of Jesus Christ through the will of God ... unto the church of God which is at Corinth, to them that are sanctified in Christ Jesus, called to be saints, with all that in every place call upon the name of Jesus Christ our Lord, both their's and our's...."*

Without Paul there would be no epistle to many of the churches of the New Testament; no letter to the church at Rome in which he declared himself to be *"a servant of Jesus Christ, called to be an apostle, separated unto the gospel of God"* (Rom. 1:1). There would be no letter to the churches at Galatia, in which he writes in Galatians 1:1–4, *"Paul, an apostle, (not of men, neither by man, but by Jesus Christ, and God the Father, who raised him from the dead;) and all the brethren which are with me, unto the churches of Galatia: grace be to you and peace from God the Father, and from our Lord Jesus Christ, who gave himself for our sins, that he might deliver us from this present evil world, according to the will of God and our Father."* There would be no church at Ephesus, at Philippi, or Colossae! Paul could not have written from Athens the first and second epistles to the Thessalonians. We would not have the apostolic tutelage of young pastors like Timothy, Titus, or Philemon.

As Paul carried out the ministry to which God called him, he was often imprisoned, beaten, and even left for dead. Personal sacrifice and suffering have always been the experience of those who dare to be called of God to lead His people and His church.

It goes without saying that the greatest leader of all times is Jesus, our Savior! We celebrate with awe, those feelings of reverential respect mixed with wonder! We celebrate with thanksgiving, our human expressions of extreme gratitude! We celebrate with humility,

Principle 9: Must Be Willing to Make Personal Sacrifices

a view of ourselves as being unworthy of the supreme sacrifice of our God wrapping Himself in human flesh, coming to live among us as one of us, suffering and dying for our sins. What a savior!

Church leadership must never be regarded as a "stand alone" vocation or avocation. Those who follow the call of leadership soon discover that such choice commits them, and every aspect of their life, to the effects of such choice. Leaders cannot simply go home, pull off their jacket, and sit in an easy chair as if they are done for the day. Quite the contrary, the functions of church leaders go home with them. The sacrifice of time is but the first of many sacrifices to be extracted from their personal life. A leader's time does not belong to the leader, nor his or her family! Try though they may, he or she will soon be introduced to the cycle of cancellations and rescheduling of both personal and family events as regular occurrences. Things such as vacation plans, holiday schedules, birthdays, and anniversary outings are all subject to the duties of the average church leader.

I am still pained by the vivid memories of the scheduled family vacation of 1957. My father went and purchased a new 1957 Ford Fairlane 500 for the purpose of taking the family on a West Coast vacation. Days before we were scheduled to leave, our senior pastor came to our house to speak with my dad concerning a matter involving the church. I do not know the context of their conversation, but I do know that it resulted in the cancellation of our trip. Whatever the need that necessitated the service of my father as assistant pastor, usurped the vacation. At eight years old, that event was my matriculation into the school of church leadership training. I am now completing my sixty-seventh year of leadership training.

Several years later, as an adult with the responsibilities of a family and a mortgage, I interviewed for and was offered an executive position with a national corporation that was headquartered in my home city. By the time I completed the multi-leveled interview process, I knew enough about the position to know that it would spill over into my life as an encroachment upon my ability to continue to serve the ministry to which God called me. After concluding that I would not be able to effectively fulfill the responsibilities of such a demanding executive position while fulfilling the increasing demands of ministry, I declined to accept the position along with a salary that superseded any previous salary, or any salary I had ever imagined.

While somewhat reticent at the time about the decision, God has affirmed over and over that my decision was the right decision. God's affirmation of the appropriateness of my decision has been demonstrated to my satisfaction in multiple ways, including, but not limited to, financial, professional, and ministerial. Around that time, I heard a sermon by the late Dr. Oral Roberts, who served as founding president of the Oral Roberts University. The title was, "You Can't Go Under for Coming Over to the Lord's Side!" My life has been a living confirmation of that sermon, and of God's commitment to those who commit themselves to Him.

My advice to all sincere church leaders is to follow your calling without the intimidation of feeling as if you are making bad decisions. Your all-knowing God was aware of the turns and directions of your life long before you ever realized the call to leadership upon your life. Know that God is powerful enough to work through you without hurting you or your family! Further, I urge you to act in faith as you consider the personal sacrifices you will be called upon to make; you cannot go under because you came over to the Lord's side. I urge you to read Principle 17, "Church Leaders Must be Willing to Suffer."

Church leaders must be willing to make personal sacrifices!

Principle *10*

Church Leaders Must Be Emotionally Stable

Control your temper, for anger labels you a fool.
—Ecclesiastes 7:9 (NLT)

Don't be too quick to get angry because anger lives in the fool's heart. —Ecclesiastes 7:9 (CEB)

How many times have you heard the expression, "Control your temper!"? For most of us, it seems to have been a constant refrain; repeatedly we were cautioned by parents, teachers, supervisors, and sometimes peers, to manage our emotions. While the task of managing one's emotions might seem difficult for some, it is mandatory for those spirited enough to accept the responsibility of serving as leaders in the church. This challenging task is so consequential that the future of our leadership hinges on our capability to maintain a reasonable level of emotional stability. Doing so can be relatively easy when things are going well, and we are free from life's pressure of disappointment. However, the problem surfaces when things become so out of whack that nothing seems to work according to plan. Our frustration with this type of disappointment stretches the limits of our ability to manage our emotional responses and to maintain control.

No matter how thoroughly we plan, it is not uncommon for leaders to find themselves in positions that strip them of the capacity to maintain an orderly flow of events. To some degree, it is understandable that a leader's temper may flare during the heat of pressure brought on by such frustrations. However, leadership decorum demands that some display of dignity remains evident as we manage such moments. When leaders experience emotional meltdowns in reaction to the disarray of things going out of control, they must still exhibit a level of calmness in the presence of those whom he or she is charged with leading.

Apostle Paul addressed the Corinthian church concerning the confusion and disorder that takes place during a service when multiple people attempt to prophesy at the same time. I would like to borrow Paul's admonition in verse 32. Even though I am deliberately removing the statement from its original context, the overtones remain applicable to the disorder caused when leaders fail to display emotional stability during times of crisis. Paul reminded the church that *"the spirits of the prophets are subject to the prophets"* (1 Cor. 14:32).

Emotional instability can be the result of several factors that may come to play in the psyche of a leader who finds himself in problematic situations where control is absent. This is especially true when the absence of control is the result of circumstances outside of the domain of the leader. An example of such occasion could be a sudden downpour of rain during an outside outing. For the purpose of this example, we will stipulate that the leader showed extreme diligence in the planning of the event; the weather forecast for the day of the event was checked multiple times. Additional weather checks were performed the day before and the morning of the event; the forecast was clear. As an added precaution, tents were ordered as backups in the event of an unexpected shift in the weather. The event started; the set-ups were completed; all was well! Suddenly, out of nowhere, it started raining like a coastal hurricane was imminent! As the crew hurried to set up the tents, they discovered that the mechanism that allowed the tents to open and close was defective. The frustration of the rains ruining the set-ups and the event, and the frustration of the tents not engaging as anticipated caused an even higher level of immediate anxiety in the leader. But, in situations like this, an effective leader is expected to display a calmness that demonstrates a measure of emotional stability.

As church leaders, we must occasionally examine ourselves in an effort to ascertain if we continue to possess the ability to remain visibly calm in a highly charged atmosphere of unpredictable disruptions. Failure to do so could subject reticent leaders to displays of emotional havoc at times when the future of our leadership success is in the balance.

Again, emotional instability can be the result of several factors coming to play in the psyche of leaders when we find ourselves in situations where control is absent. Let's examine some of those factors. Among the most common are depression, genetics, borderline personality disorder, prior trauma, anxiety disorder, abusive relationships, environmental factors, substance abuse, medication, alcohol misuse, and even cardiovascular disease. Needless to say, the list goes on and on. As can be imagined, the affected leaders may not even be aware that they suffer from such conditions. Often, causes such as early childhood trauma, or previous substance or alcohol abuse, may have taken place during a time in life when church leadership, or the church itself, was not a consideration.

I am the first to admit that I am not clinically qualified to diagnose Emotionally Unstable Personality Disorder (EUPD). Years of leadership experience at multiple levels, and my experience of managing leaders, have trained me to identify symptoms suggestive of

EUPD. Symptoms such as: chronic anger at small matters, frequent mood swings, excessive impulsivity, aggravated fear of abandonment, chronic bouts of irritability, extreme anxiety, and heightened suspicions of strangers are all suggestive of character traits of suffering from EUPD. Any of these factors can cause a level of stress that lends itself to emotional instability.

These factors can be managed, controlled, and eliminated! Clinicians have found success in natural remedies such as exercise, proper diet, adequate sleep, daily rest and relaxation, etc. These methods may be extremely helpful to the stress-filled life of church leaders. I also suggest daily prayer, Bible reading, meditation, and routine counseling with senior leaders, along with faithful attendance with attentive listening to Sunday morning worship and weekly Bible study. While leaders are indispensable to the success of any church or church-related institution, emotionally stable leaders are more indispensable to the spiritual growth of church members!

Church leaders must be emotionally stable!

Principle *11*

Church Leaders Must Be Financially Responsible

But if any provide not for his own, and specially for those of his own house, he hath denied the faith, and is worse than an infidel. —1 Timothy 5:8

In 1 Timothy 5, Apostle Paul gives pastoral care guidance to Timothy, his son in ministry. As we read the text, it is apparent that Timothy is a church leader. Paul instructs him on how he is to treat the various categories of members. Paul shifts to the responsibilities of individual family members for each other, specifically as it relates to widowed mothers. He even goes so far as to highlight the responsibility of children and grandchildren to their aged parents. In verse 4, he writes, *"But if a particular widow has children or grandchildren, they should first learn to respect their own family and repay their parents, because this pleases God"* (1 Tim. 5:4 CEB).

In verse 7, Paul makes a statement that must ring out in the hearts and minds of today's church leaders. He said, *"Teach these things so that the families will be without fault"* (CEB).

As we read the entire text, we will understand the necessity of being responsible in all aspects of life. However, it tends to show much more dramatically in the area of financial responsibility, since the results of financial irresponsibility cannot be hidden from those around us. It announces itself in our inability to maintain the things necessary to live successfully. It drives some into areas of activity that are blatantly inconsistent with the kind of lifestyle that pleases God. Stealing, cheating, and lying are but the tip of the iceberg of possibilities of the desperately impoverished. I am by no means suggesting that every person who becomes a victim of extreme financial hardship resorts to scandalous practices; there are those who maintain spiritual integrity in moments of extreme economic difficulties.

Several years ago, I worked as a personnel director (now referred to as a human resource manager) for a medium-size business of less than two hundred employees. I was responsible for hiring personnel at all levels of employment. While all positions required some type of background investigation, some positions required more extensive investigations than others. Applicants applying for positions that involved fiduciary responsibilities, or management of departments or personnel that handled money or inventory, had to pass a criminal background check and a seven-year credit check. If any of these investigations, especially the credit check, raised "red flags" of any sort, we would not hire such person. Our company's philosophy was that applicants experiencing financial problems would be more apt to steal than those whose financial capacity was not in jeopardy.

Any person may be subject to adverse economic conditions that may erupt in a given community from time to time; he can find himself in financial disarray through no fault of his own. However, more often than not, many financial difficulties arise as a result of financial mismanagement. In many years of pastoring and training pastors, I have found that the primary cause of financial difficulties in the local church is often the result of financial mismanagement as well. One culprit is overspending! As the leader of an auxiliary within a local church, or the senior pastor who leads the entire church, you must be able to reconcile the relationship between income and expenses. You will need to have a system in place to readily identify the difference between projected income and actual income. And, of course, you'll need to do the same thing for expenditures—projected expenditures versus actual expenditures. At no point does a prudent leader operate solely based on projected income without monitoring such income along the way and reconciling it against actual expenditures. A prudent leader must take into consideration the historical record of actual income. What have we done in the past three to five years?

Another culprit on the road to financial mismanagement is the tendency to either fail to keep good financial records, or failure to monitor the financial records kept. While it is easy to understand how financial records show where we have been, we must also understand that good financial records show where we are going as well.

After retiring from almost forty years of pastoring, and fifteen years of serving the bishopric, my wife and I bought a forty-two-foot diesel RV. We have since driven it all over the country, from coast to coast and border to border. We have driven to faraway places where we had never gone and had little knowledge of how to get there. The only guidance we had was our Global Positioning System (GPS), which allowed us to find our way around with turn-by-turn accuracy. I pity the driver who sets out on a cross-country trip without the aid of a map or GPS guidance!

Just as GPS guidance is necessary to successful RV travels, budgetary controls are essential to the success of the church, and any auxiliary within the church. Those same principles must be applied to the management of a leader's individual income and expenditures.

How leaders manage their own finances tells a great deal about the character of the leader. A leader's character can either catapult him to the apex of successful leadership or drag him to the nadir of dismal failure. Unfortunately, the one thing some leaders never seem to realize is that leadership is not about the leader; rather, it's about those being led. Therefore, failure must never be an option for those called into the leadership of the church, or any aspect of the church. Those who are courageous enough to accept the challenge of church leadership must, at the same time, be courageous enough to meet the challenge!

Apostle Paul makes an interesting observation in the text shared at the beginning of this lesson: *"But if any provide not for his own, and specially for those of his own house, he hath denied the faith, and is worse than an infidel."*

Paul is saying, in essence, that the leader who fails to take financial responsibility has denied the faith and is worse than an infidel. Albeit, in this case, he's referring to leaders of the family. Conversely, we can very easily apply his profound observation to leaders in and of the church, and any organization related to the church. An irresponsible leader has denied his faith and is worse than an infidel. I find it quite intriguing that Paul used the word "infidel," because this three-syllable word denotes one who is not faithful. *"In"* denotes "not"; *"fidelis"* denotes "faithful"—archaic definitions speak to one who no longer believes in the inspiration of the Scriptures. This is important because if a leader is to maintain a viable relationship with God, he must constantly feed on the inspiration of Scripture—Scripture *"given by the inspiration of God, and is profitable for doctrine, for reproof, for correction, for instruction in righteousness"* (2 Tim. 3:16).

A faithful and conscientious church leader thrives on a relationship with Scripture. To abandon that relationship is to abandon the

Principle 11: Must Be Financially Responsible

predominant source of daily inspiration and reinforcement. It is no secret that, in addition to prayer, God works through the agency of Scripture, from which the voice of God is revealed. From that voice, leaders find the pathway to the will of God, and the capacity to please God. Not only must church leaders strive to please God in every aspect of their leadership responsibility, but they do also not want to be classified as infidels.

Church leaders must be financially responsible!

A leader's character can either catapult him to the apex of successful leadership or drag him to the nadir of dismal failure.

Principle 12

Church Leaders Must Be Willing to Interact with Peers

May the God who gives endurance and encouragement give you the same attitude of mind toward each other that Christ Jesus had. —Romans 15:5

Rebuke not an elder, but intreat him as a father; and the younger men as brethren; the elder women as mothers; the younger as sisters, with all purity. —1 Timothy 5:1–2

L et's start this session with a challenging quote from the late Jim Rohn, an internationally acclaimed author and motivational speaker, who wrote: "The challenge of leadership is to be strong, but not rude; be kind, but not weak; be bold, but not bully; be thoughtful, but not lazy; be humble, but not timid; be proud, but not arrogant; have humor, but without folly."[2]

It is commonly agreed that the process of learning involves far more than academic instructions or attending the great institutions of learning. Obviously, formal matriculation is not necessarily the

---

2   Rohn, J, (2012). *My Philosophy for Successful Living.* No Dream too Big LLC.

bedrock of learning. One of the earliest recognized learning processes for human beings is peer association. In fact, sociologists argue that, for some, what is learned through peer interactions can be more effective than learning in a classroom setting. One of the foremost disciplines learned through peer interaction is what social psychology refers to as social skills. An inordinate deficit of such skills can render a person incapable of maintaining effective interactions with others. Not only is this a most undesirable position for church leaders, but it is also not a good position for people in general—churched or unchurched.

Social skills learned through peer interactions enable peers to communicate with each other in an appropriate manner—ways necessary for getting along harmoniously. It can be argued that positive peer interactions aid in building the character traits essential to successful church leadership. One much needed character trait is the ability to act in ways that demonstrate a caring disposition. Other usable traits, which can be learned through peer interactions, are fairness, respectfulness, trustworthiness, and responsibility. Each of which contributes to a person's ability to maintain healthy relationships beyond such person's peer base. A deficiency in those areas will almost always display itself as negative thinking and substandard behavior; the results of which will be magnified by the position of church leadership.

The most impending danger of a lack of peer interaction is the passive development of anti-social behavior. While such behavior is sometimes considered psychopathic, at the very least, it is potentially dangerous. Its propensity for harm to others is heightened when such behavior is part of the psychological profile of a church leader. For leaders interested in a broader look at the negative implications of such behavior, especially when manifested in situations where group dynamics are at play, I recommend a book written by Robert D. Hare, titled, *Snakes in Suits: When Psychopaths Go to Work.* In this book, published in 2006, Hare, a criminal psychologist, teams up with Paul Babiak, an industrial psychologist. Together they take a riveting look at the dangers of engaging persons who significantly lack the moral compass brought about by positive social skills and strong peer interactions. The discussions include the negative results of such persons engaging in leadership functions within a group setting. Babiak and Hare describe how a typical psychopath climbs to and maintains power within such setting. They describe such persons thusly:

> Many traits exhibited by these individuals include superficial charm, insincerity, egocentricity, lack of empathy, manipulativeness, grandiosity, low agreeableness, independence, rigidity, stubbornness, and dictatorial tendencies.[3]

The sad irony is that when such persons are engaged in the leadership of the church, these same characteristics can be identified. Please note the admonition of Principle 21, "Church Leaders Must Be Spirit-Filled!" I must caution you, however, that unless church leaders allow the Holy Spirit to do the work necessary in bringing about *"the work of grace,"* the leaders will show little to no transformation of character or moral compass. It is not enough to merely be filled with the Holy Spirit; one must live in obedience to the guidance and transformative power of the Holy Spirit! Church leaders must become one with the admonition of Apostle Paul to the church at Philippi, as he urged them in Philippians 2:1–4:

> *If there be therefore any consolation in Christ, if any comfort of love, if any fellowship of the Spirit, if any bowels and mercies, fulfil ye my joy, that ye be likeminded, having the same love, being of one accord, of one*

---

3   Hare, R.D., (2006). *Snakes in Suits: When Psychopaths Go to Work*. Harper Business

mind. Let nothing be done through strife or vainglory; but in lowliness of mind let each esteem other better than themselves. Look not every man on his own things, but every man also on the things of others.

Paul went on to say in verse 5: *"Let this mind be in you, which was also in Christ Jesus."* In verse 7, Christ is described by Paul as follows: *"...but made himself of no reputation, and took upon him the form of a servant."*

I further remind you of Paul's encouragement to the saints at Rome, to whom he wrote in Romans 15:5, *"May the God who gives endurance and encouragement give you the same attitude of mind toward each other that Christ Jesus had."*

In the many leadership seminars I have been called upon and blessed to conduct during the past several years, I have made a distinct point of reminding leaders that, in addition to the reasons stated in this work, it is absolutely necessary to establish a peer group of "like leaders" with whom to chat, consult, and have general conversations, both formally and informally throughout the tenure of their leadership. This provides each leader in the group the availability of the experience of other leaders who wrestle with similar issues. This also provides a forum within which leaders can express thoughts and ideas while enjoying freedom from ridicule or negative dispositions. Peer interactions serve as a grounding mechanism for active leaders; this aids leaders in the necessary, but often neglected, challenge to remain practical in their approaches to the various temptations of leadership. My use of the word "temptations" speaks to both a leader's innate tendency to treat new ideas as if they are infallible, and the possibility of any nefarious activity that may invade such leader's space from time to time. In addition, temptation also speaks to the egotistically driven self-perceptions that so easily beset us as leaders, and thus, make it impossible to run this race of a successful leadership experience with ample patience and humility. For to perform in any other way negates the God-quality of church leadership and renders the church leader psychopathic to the degree that even in the church, we will witness "snakes in suits."

Church leaders must be willing to interact with peers!

It is not enough to merely be filled with the Holy Spirit; one must live in obedience to the guidance and transformative power of the Holy Spirit!

Principle *13*

Church Leaders Must Be Flexible

Now I beseech you, brethren, by the name of our Lord Jesus Christ, that ye all speak the same thing, and that there be no divisions among you; but that ye be perfectly joined together in the same mind and in the same judgment.
— 1 Corinthians 1:10

It is not uncommon for groups of people from the same environment to disagree adamantly about an issue that seems to an outsider to be of little to no importance. I have seen such disagreements become so intense that the ensuing arguments caused such strong riffs between group members that it resulted in permanent divisions between people who had worked together for years prior to the onset of the disagreement. While we would like to think of the church as being different than secular organizations, it is not when it comes to the blending of human personalities! I must confess that one would expect that there would be a difference in how church members respond to internal disagreements. Unfortunately, human nature often overrides spiritual nature.

When lay members behave meanly towards each other, it often causes a disturbance to the "bond of fellowship" that makes the church desirably unique. But, when church leaders are at odds with those whom they are responsible for leading, it not only disrupts the atmosphere of the biblically-required coexistence necessary for a healthy church, but it also creates "church hurt" in those who are often the church's most vulnerable. For this reason, many churches unnecessarily lose potentially good members. The sad reality is that, in many cases, the interactions that caused the church hurt were of little to no importance. In a majority of cases, it was just a matter of human pride that interrupted the leader's ability to think in a godly manner.

Church leaders must work to eliminate the egomaniacal pride that pushes them into the corner of irresponsible behavior. Such pride produces an inflexibility that makes them as difficult to get along with as for a *"camel to go through the eye of a needle"* (Matt. 19:24). As is the case in almost any emotional imbalance, such pride is a "trick of the devil." It's just another tool in Satan's arsenal of weapons against the church. The shame is that it is often launched through the personality of church leaders—those to whom lay members look to for guidance in their walk with God.

Inflexibility is a state of rigidity that renders us incapable of compromising. Inflexible leaders are often unwilling to change; such unwillingness can be evidenced in their attitudes, personalities, and responses to suggestions that are contrary to their positions in matters of church and life in general. The unwillingness of inflexibility prevents the affected leaders from embracing any initiative except those which coincide with their point of view. In defense of their stiffness, such leaders often become combatively dogmatic to the point that ideas held are presented as if they were incontrovertible truths. The problem is that often the small measure of truth that might be evident in such positions is eroded by the lack of flexibility in the defense of their positions.

It is noteworthy to mention that just as senseless moments of disagreement among church members often capture the headlines in today's assemblies of believers, they also arose in the church at Corinth, and other New Testament venues. Pastors and overseers have long struggled to quiet such outbreaks. Apostle Paul can be heard pleading to the church concerning the necessity of brothers and sisters in Christ to agree. He wrote in 1 Corinthians 1:10 (ESV), *"I appeal to you, brothers, by the name of our Lord Jesus Christ, that all of you agree, and that there be no divisions among you, but that you be united in the same mind and the same judgment."*

While the inflexibility of church leaders may not have been the direct result of an identifiable disagreement, it certainly added fuel to the fire. People will disagree! Whenever more than one person is involved in a situation, the possibility of discord exists. In fact, the existence of just one person can result in discord; doctors call it "schizophrenia." It exists when a person is in mental conflict with himself. It is a disorder that affects his capacity to think clearly—a disorder that, if not properly treated, can ultimately affect how the person feels and behaves. The person might look normal and behave normal, but could lose his mental balance at any moment. He becomes mentally disoriented to the point that he literally fights himself.

While there is no such group diagnosis for a church, the results can appear the same when spiritually compromised leaders lack adequate flexibility, but fail to solicit the help of the Holy Spirit and other experienced leaders. The term "spiritually compromised leaders" does not suggest that leaders are unsaved or in a backslidden condition; quite the contrary, I am suggesting that all persons, leaders or laity, who refuse to *"yield your members as instruments of righteousness unto God"* can become targets for Satan's attempts to undermine the church through the use of unsuspecting and unconsecrated church leaders. It is ironic that in Romans 6:13, we find that the opposite of yielding to God is stated as: *"Neither yield ye your members as instruments of unrighteousness unto sin."*

Rather than allowing contentious disagreements to fester into full-scale division, leaders must demonstrate the level of godly flexibility that is implicit in the instructions of Jesus in Mark 11:25–26: *"And when ye stand praying, forgive, if ye have ought against any: that your Father also which is in heaven may forgive you your trespasses. But if ye do not forgive, neither will your Father which is in heaven forgive your trespasses."*

Jesus's instructions to forgive displays a level of spirituality that must be depicted in the attitude and disposition of all church leaders. As an added benefit, Jesus reminds us that by following His recipe for the peaceful coexistence of members and leaders, compliant leaders put themselves in position to be forgiven by God when moments of trespass interrupt their otherwise peaceful lives.

Church leaders must be flexible!

Principle 14

Church Leaders Must Be Socially Responsible

For one believeth that he may eat all things: another, who is weak, eateth herbs. Let not him that eateth despise him that eateth not; and let not him which eateth not judge him that eateth: for God hath received him.... Let us not therefore judge one another any more: but judge this rather, that no man put a stumblingblock or an occasion to fall in his brother's way.... But if thy brother be grieved with thy meat, now walkest thou not charitably. Destroy not him with thy meat, for whom Christ died.... It is good neither to eat flesh, nor to drink wine, nor any thing whereby thy brother stumbleth, or is offended, or is made weak.
—Romans 14:2–3, 13, 15, 21

But take heed lest by any means this liberty of yours become a stumblingblock to them that are weak.... Wherefore, if meat make my brother to offend, I will eat no flesh while the world standeth, lest I make my brother to offend.
—1 Corinthians 8:9, 13

A dear colleague of mine once reminded me that if one wishes to have friends, he must be willing to accept their varying personalities no matter how different they are. Cardinal rules for social engagement must include the ability to accept others at whatever state of development, or lack thereof, they may be. The greatest disservice we can do to another person is to try to change him or her for our personal benefit. We often see this in husband and wife relationships; it rarely works there, and even less in other relationships. As church leaders, you must understand that every person has the inherent right to be who he or she is. The need for change in a person's life, or way of thinking, is not the question; however, it is not the church leader's responsibility to change a follower's personality. Effective leaders seek to positively influence followers to the degree that their followers will themselves wish to change, and thus, seek to initiate the needed change. John Quincy Adams once said, "If your actions inspire others to dream more, learn more, do more, and become more, you are a leader." Of course, it goes without saying that the converse is equally true.

Social responsibility in church leadership is a term that conveys how church leaders must act in order to benefit the church and those who are responsive to such leadership. Social responsibility suggests both the kinds of things leaders must do, and those things leaders are prohibited from doing; all of which is for the betterment of the institution in which they lead. As social responsibility in general must seek to ground all actions and decisions in firm ethical practices, social responsibility in regard to church leadership must seek both ethical and biblical foundations upon which to base all actions and decisions. To act in a way that is either unethical or unbiblical is, for church leaders, tantamount to acting socially irresponsibly. The Apostle Paul wrote to the church leaders of the church at Rome, *"We do not live for ourselves only, and we do not die for ourselves only"* (Rom. 14:7 GNT).

Principle 14: Must Be Socially Responsible

While there is a plethora of issues that determine the level of social responsibility practiced by church leaders, I shall seek to discuss only two such issues in today's lesson. One matter of discussion is regarding rules about behavior in the church community. Even though there is not a "book of etiquette" on how church leaders are to behave socially, the Bible is rather comprehensive in such regard. The second area of discussion deals with a church leader's actions in the company of others. My concern is that all activities, including those intended for pleasure, will be conducted in a manner that is doctrinally, biblically, and socially acceptable. My focus is not on a list of socially responsible activities; instead, I will look at two principles that convey such responsibility at an extraordinary level.

Amid much banter about responsibility *to*, and responsibility *for*, our brothers and sisters in Christ, Apostle Paul lays down a major principle of social responsibility by admonishing the saints at Rome: *"Let us therefore follow after the things which make for peace, and things wherewith one may edify another"* (Rom. 14:19).

This principle does not merely deal with small matters of polite discussion; it establishes an ever-present attitude within which all activity and communications among members of the church at all levels must be conducted. It spells out the tone of leader/follower interactions, as well as that of member-to-member dialogue and activities.

There was much discussion in the early New Testament church about what could be eaten and what was not allowable. There were members on both sides of this discussion whose objective was to otherwise maintain a good working relationship with each other. As a leader of the church, one of Paul's responsibilities was to maintain an environment within which both sides could continue in the fellowship of the church as they followed the leading of their own conscience. You might notice that Paul raised the issue that since this was not a question of salvation, or that would become a hindrance to salvation, a decision on either side should not impede the member's ability to work in harmony with each other. There was not an unethical side to this question! There was no unbiblical side to this question! There was no breach of theology, systematic or otherwise, to this question. It was a matter of choice based upon the development of each person's conscience.

Paul respected the liberty of thought and actions developed in the spiritual growth of some of his followers. He acknowledged others who, while in the same church, had not grown to the same level, or at the same pace. Because of that, he encouraged the more consciously developed followers that they must not allow their liberty to harm those who did not enjoy such liberty. He proclaimed at one point that if eating meat offended his brother, then he would not eat meat. What an unselfish and godly approach to the social responsibility of a leader's concern for the spiritual well-being of his followers.

Church leaders must learn to exercise the same level of care for those whom they are charged with leading. Whether it is a disagreement among some followers, or a more serious disagreement between follower and leader, the right to live out the restraints of their own conscience is the right of every member of every church, so long as their restraints do not violate biblical or doctrinal principles of the church or church organization in question.

I recall as a young minister how vexed I was that my brothers and sisters of another church could not quite understand one of the major doctrinal issues of the church in which I was raised. My spirit was grieved to the point that I went before the Lord in sincere prayer in my effort to reconcile the error of my brothers and sisters. I was awed by the fact that, as I prayed for guidance, the Holy Spirit spoke into my heart words of assurance that allowed me to understand that the same God who is concerned about and directs my affairs, is also concerned about and gives directions to the affairs of my disagreeing brothers and sisters. While the disagreement still exists, my feelings of consternation and aggravation have ceased to exist. All of us are now senior saints and senior leaders; we are still brothers and sisters in Christ who still find enjoyment in friendly interactions when we occasionally run into each other. By their response to such matters, church leaders can either enhance the fellowship of members, or completely destroy any possibility of fellowship among members. It's all a matter of how leaders handle social responsibilities in matters of dispute.

Church leaders must be socially responsible!

Church leadership must seek both ethical and biblical foundations upon which to base all actions and decisions.

Principle 15

Church Leaders Must Be Intellectually Astute

And this I pray, that your love may abound yet more and more in knowledge and in all judgment.—Philippians 1:9

Behold, I send you forth as sheep in the midst of wolves: be ye therefore wise as serpents, and harmless as doves.
—Matthew 10:16

To some degree every person is endowed with the capacity to process the various nuances of life. The extent of such capacity varies from person to person. It is not prejudicial to acknowledge that some people have a greater ability to reason than others. The same is true when we measure the objectivity level of any group of people. As we move from person to person, we discover that people's ability to understand the facets of life is often not congruent. Even when such movement stays within the same group, there can still be a great disparity between one person's level of understanding as opposed to another's. This is what the intellect is all about; a person's intellect determines his ability to reason, understand, and think objectively.

To the extent that a person's life remains uncomplicated, the person can have a somewhat normal life despite having to deal with the challenges of a lack of intellectual capacity. The problem is, however, that simplicity of life is never a guaranteed factor of life. Life does get complicated from time to time. During those periods of complication, people need the intellectual ability to understand, think, and make rational decisions. In all cases, that capacity depends upon the progression of a person's ability to think and acquire sufficient knowledge. His thinking and acquisition of knowledge must rise to the level of the complication, if he is to meet the challenges of life. The difference between being able to understand, and thus, resolve life's problems, is the difference in intellectual capacities. This is an area where spiritually mature church leaders can be of great assistance to the shortfalls of their followers.

Among the factors to be considered as senior leaders seeking to fulfill the leadership needs of the church is intellectual capacity. The value of appointing church leaders who are intellectually astute is unquestionably beneficial to the church, and to those who follow their leadership. What value is there in appointing leaders who lack the ability to process the complex issues that often arise during the course of the daily business of the church, its departments, or its members? Even if the business is not complex, the lack of the capacity of followers to understand logical solutions often creates complexities.

In addition to the day-to-day logistical concerns, church leaders must be able to face problems, evaluate problems, understand the ramifications suggested by problems, create solutions that will solve the problems, and communicate those solutions to the followers. This process can be better handled by those who have acquired an adequate level of intellectual astuteness. Astuteness means to possess the innate ability to accurately assess contemporary situations and mitigate any damage they could cause; it further means to have the ability to transform those situations from a potential disadvantage to an advantage.

Principle 15: Must Be Intellectually Astute

Success in attaining higher education or advanced degrees does not correspondingly result in intellectual astuteness. I have encountered professionals with "legitimately" earned master's and doctorate degrees, who, while successful in their field of study, were definitively simple when faced with issues outside of their field of study. Like many other capacities held by seemingly unlikely persons, intellectual astuteness is often a gift of God given without regard to the person's propensity for formal education. Indeed, it would appear that the optimum candidates for church leadership are persons who are both formally educated and naturally gifted with intellectual astuteness. But, since, as stated in another principle, "Church Leaders Must be Chosen by God," when that principle is followed, we need not worry about the mental capacity of our God-chosen leaders.

Even though all God-qualified church leaders are fully capable of commanding all applicable responsibilities of their position, I must address the reality that there are church leaders who, though qualified, are often negligent in the performance of their duties to the degree that their leadership is essentially ineffective. It appears that the functions of leadership, like so many other operations within the church, have been redefined by cultural practices that are no more a part of the church than the devil himself. It reminds me of the painful demise of preaching in today's church as opposed to its purpose when described in Old Testament Scripture:

> *So they read in the book in the law of God distinctly, and gave the sense, and caused them to understand the reading.* (Neh. 8:8)

It is glaringly apparent that the purpose of preaching was to give the sense of the Word of God, and to cause the people to understand it. In other words, preaching was designed to explain, or exegete, the Scripture. This is a perfectly logical assessment of the preaching of the gospel, because the gospel is the power of God unto the salvation.

> *For I am not ashamed of the gospel of Christ: for it is the power of God unto salvation to every one that believeth; to the Jew first, and also to the Greek.* (Rom. 1:16)

Please understand that the gospel is not confined to the events of the New Testament; but rather, the gospel is the presentation of the entire narrative of God in Christ Jesus. While that narrative is contained in, and is presented by the whole of Scripture, it begins with Genesis 1:1: *"In the beginning God created the heaven and the earth."*

I have observed the drastic change in the purpose of preaching by virtue of the fact that I hear so many sermons that are void of any attempt to explain a single Scripture, including the text from which the sermon was preached. During the period of my career when I taught preaching, I often reminded the young seminarians that the preaching must always include some exegesis of the text or the context from which the sermon is raised. Failure to include some sense of the text strips the presentation of any sermonic value.

I raise that issue because, in like manner, church leaders are facing an evolution of principles in all areas of church dynamics; the ways in which followers now relate to leaders illustrate a great departure from the historical evidence of leader/member relations. Leaders in today's church must be able to quickly assess and process weighty information—information that is sometimes beyond the realm of reasonability. And, in some cases, leaders must almost instantly formulate a plan of action. I agree that leaders must rely on the Holy Spirit, the leading of the Lord, and the counsel of senior leaders; however, I also believe that leaders, and the church, would be greatly benefited by the gift of God in the area of intellectual ingenuity. Intellectually astute church leaders would be of tremendous benefit to the people of God by being able to provide a level of care that could ward off much of the destructive rhetoric that infiltrates its ranks. It becomes a modern-day example of the shepherd, David, protecting the sheep from the intrusion of the dangerous lion and bear. *"And David said unto Saul, Thy servant kept his father's sheep, and there came a lion, and a bear, and took a lamb out of the flock: and I went out after him, and smote him, and delivered it out of his mouth"* (1 Sam. 17:34–35).

Church leaders must be intellectually astute!

If You Are Enjoying This Book, Will You Help Me Spread the Word?

There are several ways you can help me get the word out about the message of this book…

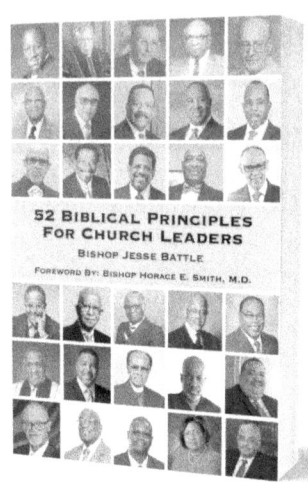

- Visit my website, and leave a review: 52principlesforchurchleaders. com

- Recommend the book to friends and fellow church leaders. Word of mouth is still the more effective form of advertising.

- Purchase additional copies to give away as gifts.

- Post a 5-Star review on Amazon, Goodreads and other places that come to mind.

- Write about the book on your Facebook, Twitter, Instagram, Google+, any social media sites you regularly use.

- Post a photo of yourself with the book on your social media.

- Ask bookstores if they carry the book. If not, they can easily order it through all major distributors.

- If you blog, consider referencing the book, or publishing an excerpt from the book with a link back to the website where you bought it.

- Do you know a podcaster, journalist or media personality who might be willing to interview me or write an article based on the book?

- Contact me by email at 52principlesbook@gmail.com.

Principle 16

Church Leaders Must Be Lovers of the People of God

We've done this since we heard of your faith in Christ Jesus and your love for all God's people. You have this faith and love because of the hope reserved for you in heaven. You previously heard about this hope through the true message, the good news. —Colossians 1:4–5 (CEB)

In the above text, Apostle Paul commended the members and leaders of the Colossian church for their love for the people of God. This is extremely noteworthy, because it is one of the basic requirements for anyone who seeks to concern himself with the well-being of others in any area of life. To truly care for other people, caregivers must have positive feelings about the people cared for, if the caregiver wishes to achieve the maximum influence on the lives of the people for which he or she is charged with caring. I have seen countless instances where someone pretended to serve as a caregiver to those for whom, in reality, he or she had little to no concern. I have also witnessed the scars left upon those being cared for because of the negative feelings of the caregivers towards them. Believe me, if you are going to become an effective leader, you must love the people you are charged with leading. There is an adage that says, "No one cares how much you know, until they know how much you care."

According to *National Geographic*, canines possess the ability to "pick up" their owner's emotions; they can sense how their owner feels about them. This capacity in human beings has been the subject of debate over the years. Some scientists argue that people are also gifted with the natural tendency to sense what others feel about them just from watching their actions and reactions. Many scientists who support such notions also believe that the human brain is equipped with what is often referred to as "mirror neurons," which are brain cells that are activated as a person watches the actions of another. Some scientists assert that the same observations can be made by a person watching his own actions as well.

While the basic context of the interpretation of the feelings of others is referred to as empathy, modern researchers have determined that two types of empathy are generally active in the brain cells of most human beings. These two empathies allow the cognitive determination of the feelings of others. "Affective empathy" speaks to the perception we often get in response to the emotions of others towards us; whereas "cognitive empathy" speaks to our capacity to identify, understand, and categorize those emotions. Albeit, it is widely accepted in the scientific community that people do possess the ability to sense what others feel about and towards them. While I am neither a psychologist nor sociologist, and, as such, cannot authenticate the accuracy of the above stated information, I have been blessed with many years of leadership experience within the context of the church. I have been able to document from my own observation, and the countless hours I've spent counseling others about their feelings, that there is a measure of practical truth concerning this matter. However, despite the percentages leaning either way, a safe position is to err on the side of caution. As such, I strongly recommend that those who accept the challenge of church leadership should anticipate that the projection of their feelings, as perceived by others, could provide some indication of how the leader feels towards his or her followers.

Principle 16: Must Be Lovers of the People of God

It stands to reason that when a follower senses any disingenuous feelings on the part of leadership, he or she immediately discredits the leader. Usually, the result of a discredited leader is the tendency to follow from afar, if at all. Such actions limit the ability to provide effective leadership. While the leader may do all the right things, his or her leadership remains ineffective because the followers lack the necessary confidence to render it effective. A dear colleague, who has since gone on to be with the Lord, cautioned me many years ago that if a person accepts the challenge of leadership, he must be willing to contend with the several personalities of his followers. The effective leader must be able to do so in an unbiased fashion!

My immediate response to the advice of my colleague was that it should not be difficult to contend with those difficult personalities in light of the fact that the love of Christ is shed abroad in our lives. Little did I grasp at that time the magnitude of his advice! As the scope of my leadership experience broadened, I soon realized the extent of the problem I faced. Finally, after years of prayerful reflection and consultation with more experienced leaders, God blessed me to be able to set aside the negative inhibitions that prevented me from becoming an effective leader. I encourage those who wrestle with the human tendency of casting your negative opinions onto others to do as I did. First, prayerfully allow God to make of you that which He has called you to become: a great leader within His church. Secondly, allow the more experienced leaders around you to share the many experiences of the development of their leadership skills. As you know, we are strengthened through the testimonies of others.

Please know that God did not allow you to be selected, or elected, into leadership without first equipping you with the grace necessary for your success. Remember the words of God to Apostle Paul as he wrestled with the thorn in his flesh. God said to him, *"My grace is sufficient for thee: for my strength is made perfect in weakness"* (2 Cor. 12:9).

As leaders in the Lord's church, His grace is as available to you as for Paul during his leadership days. God's strength is as perfect for you as for church leaders across the centuries. God bestows upon those who lead His people a vast capacity to love His people. Please, open your heart so that the love of God may penetrate every corner and crevice thereof. For in doing so, you will be able to tap into the boundless love which transforms us into the successful leaders that God has called us to become. After all, we are called to be the leaders of the Lord's church!

Church leaders must be lovers of the people of God!

Principle 17

Church Leaders Must Be Willing to Suffer

But the God of all grace, who hath called us unto his eternal glory by Christ Jesus, after that ye have suffered a while, make you perfect, stablish, strengthen, settle you. To him be glory and dominion for ever and ever. Amen.
                                                    —1 Peter 5:10–11

Forasmuch then as Christ hath suffered for us in the flesh, arm yourselves likewise with the same mind.
                                                    —1 Peter 4:1

What appears to be the glamour of leadership has caused many young people to target the idea of leadership as their life's ambition. As a result, the path to leadership has become the route of travel for men and women of all walks of life. For some, the type of leadership to which they aspire has been secondary to the idea of leadership in general. While I must admit, in some fields of endeavor, being a leader does offer extraordinary levels of excitement; but for those who dare dream of leadership in the service of the church, the flavor of such leadership is quite different from that of many businesses, of politics, of education, or of medicine and law. Church leadership stands distinctly in a class all by itself. Of course, there are many similar, and even overlapping, principles that govern all leadership disciplines; but, even with that observation, church leadership stands alone.

In the humble opinion of this writer, I caution those whose ambition is to serve as leaders in the church. Such service is always inclusive of some degree of "qualifying" human suffering! Such suffering may not always be physical; rather, it may come in one of several forms. For me, it was the loss of a dearly beloved wife on a desolate stretch of a lonely Mississippi highway in the heat of the scorching August sun; it was a debilitating bout with an aggressive form of cancer whose radiation treatment fused together several internal organs of my body, all of which had to be surgically separated; it was a four-point aneurysm of the brain, about which I have been informed by leading medical authorities that no medical records exist of any person surviving an aneurysm from which blood gushed at four corners of the brain, until it was saturated in blood.

For some of my colleagues, it may have been the sudden unexplainable loss of an offspring; it may have been occupational displacement without justifying cause; it may have been the untimely loss of a residence or other assets needed to maintain their quality of life; it may have been desertion by an unfaithful spouse, or the discovery of non-monogamous behavior; it may have been the sexual realignment by an offspring; it may have been the painful estrangement, alienation, and separation of beloved family members; it may have been the amalgamation of any number of independent pain-rendering events—the "Job dilemma"! Whatever form of sacrifice or human suffering a church leader goes through, it must be acknowledged that such sacrifice is a preparatory part of the church leadership experience!

It is most disrespectful, and even negligent, of senior leaders to appoint men and women into the leadership of the church without first sharing the profound truth that intrinsic in their leadership experience will be a great deal of qualifying suffering. My use of the word "qualifying" is indeed intentional; I hold firmly to the belief that no leader can be used of God to his full capacity until such leader has gone through the refining fires of human suffering. Those whom God uses mightily are leaders who must suffer mightily! Did not Jesus proclaim in the gospel of Matthew, *"If any man will come after me, let him deny himself, and take up his cross, and follow me"* (Matt. 16:24)? Did we not hear Jesus shout out to His disciples and those who were around in the eighth chapter of Mark's gospel, *"Whosoever will come after me, let him deny himself, and take up his cross, and follow me"*?

Apostle Peter voiced his agreement with the idea of qualifying suffering in the two epistles which bear his name. He wrote in 1 Peter 5:10, *"But the God of all grace, who hath called us unto his eternal glory by Christ Jesus, after that ye have suffered a while, make you perfect, stablish, strengthen, settle you."* Notice that Peter's reference to God making one perfect, establishing, strengthening, and settling him comes only after he has suffered a while.

In 1 Peter 1:7, he talks about the trial of one's faith being much more precious than gold, a substance that no matter how valuable it becomes, will ultimately perish. Such faith, Peter asserts, even though it be tried with fire, should be found unto praise, honor, and glory! It is important to note that the use of the word "fire" in this text denotes suffering. Even though faith is tried by human suffering, it must be found unto the praise, honor, and glory of God.

Perhaps it is this undeniable and indispensable truth of the suffering of those who serve the people of God that gives clarity to the admonition contained in Romans 8:28. It is ironic that Paul prefaced verse 28 with the suggestion of verse 26, that the Spirit helps our infirmities—our physical or mental weakness. Paul writes, *"And we know that all things work together for good to them that love God, to them who are the called according to his purpose."*

Included in the context of *"all things working together"* is, of course, our suffering. Such suffering is made tolerable by our love for God; likewise, it is made redemptive by God's purpose in our calling. In other words, our level of qualifying suffering is in direct proportion to God's purpose for which we are called. Senior leaders must be willing to inform potential leaders, before they are appointed or elected to their positions as leaders, that, *"Forasmuch then as Christ hath suffered for us in the flesh, arm yourselves likewise with the same mind"* (1 Pet. 4:1).

A leader's failure to adhere to Peter's sage advice will often leave the leader marginal at best. The most likely outcome for such leader is dismal failure. While failure may be the result of willful disobedience, it could, on the other hand, be the result of passive ignorance. I'm afraid that in either case, we will end up with a failed leader and some severely injured followers. All of which could have most likely been avoided by the prudent supervision of an attentive senior leader!

There is a redemptive quality in suffering that could benefit all believers, but which must be especially appreciated by active church leaders. Paul wrote to the members of the church at Philippi about his sincere desire to have a multi-dimensional knowledge of Jesus Christ, and to be found in Him. He shared his thoughts about suffering the loss of all things for the excellency of the knowledge of Christ Jesus, his Lord. Paul continued his dialogue by asserting that he counted all things as dung that he might win Christ and be found in Him. He spoke about not having his own righteousness, but having the righteousness which is of God by faith. In verse 10 of Philippians 3, Paul pivots into sharing the reason for his profound *"relational theology"* which drove both his commitment to Christ and the leadership model conveyed to his followers: *"That I may know him, and the power of his resurrection, and the fellowship of his sufferings, being made conformable unto his death."* Knowing Christ, knowing the power of Christ's resurrection, knowing the fellowship of Christ's suffering—all of which makes Paul, and all subsequent church leaders, conformable unto Christ's death. Again, I call that "relational theology," but that's a different lesson for a different time.

One final benefit of suffering, as expressed in Paul's tutelage of Timothy, is that the pain of suffering is replaced by the joyful anticipation of reigning with Christ. Just as dying *with* Christ enrolls one into the fraternity of living *in* Christ—earthly and heavenly— suffering *with* Christ enrolls one into the kingship of Christ. In like manner, to live in a way that negates the Lordship of God in a leader's lifestyle, and leadership practices, results in God's removal of all benefits of that person's leadership.

> *It is a faithful saying: For if we be dead with him, we shall also live with him: if we suffer, we shall also reign with him: if we deny him, he also will deny us.* (2 Tim. 2:11–12)

One who leads the people of God must be willing to live in total fellowship with Jesus Christ, both in redemption and in suffering. Is not the above referenced text explicit in its suggestion that if one, as a leader in the Lord's church, suffers with Christ, such leader shall also reign with Christ?

Church leaders must be willing to suffer!

No leader can be used of God to his full capacity until such leader has gone through the refining fires of human suffering.

Principle 18

Church Leaders Must Not Have Other "gods"

I am the Lord thy God, which have brought thee out of the land of Egypt, out of the house of bondage. Thou shalt have no other gods before me. —Exodus 20:2–3

No one can serve two masters. For you will hate one and love the other; you will be devoted to one and despise the other. You cannot serve God and be enslaved to money. —Matthew 6:24 (NLT)

As one reads through the first five books of the Old Testament, known to the Greeks as the Pentateuch, and to the Jews as the Torah, he will discover several discussions of God with His people concerning their wayward tendencies of desiring and worshiping the false gods of neighboring nations. In one instance, God became so displeased by the betrayal of His people that He allowed them to be captured and oppressed for several years by their enemies. When finally, they turned to God for deliverance, He reminded them that He allowed them to be captured because they forsook Him and served other gods. At one point, God went so far as to say to them, *"Yet ye have forsaken me, and served other gods: wherefore I will deliver you no more. Go and cry unto the gods which ye have chosen; let them deliver you in the time of your tribulation"* (Judg. 10:13–14).

In yet another instance, God reminded the children of Israel that He is a jealous God. This was an expression of God's offense of Israel willingly following after idols and other representations of deities that were not reflective of the relationship that God forged with Israel. This was God's way of letting Israel know that He was jealous about both their relationship with Him and His relationship with them:

> *For thou shalt worship no other god: for the LORD, whose name is Jealous, is a jealous God.* (Exod. 34:14)

God was often angry about the illicit relationship of His people with foreign gods. New Testament writers often spoke of Israel's servitude towards these alien gods, and how such "fornication" affected Israel and their relationship with God. In all such cases, the references to other gods did indeed speak to some adopted deity created in the imagination of some mentally demented leader or people. Images of gods who, in actuality, had no God properties, including function or authority, were merely distractions of the devil designed to impede the relationship of the people of God with their God.

The mission of these distractions remains firmly attached to the original mission of Satan's exploits against God. The reference to *"other gods"* today is seated in an allegiance to other things or people that captures the interest and commitment of God's people to the point that their day-to-day living becomes excessively preoccupied with such an extraordinary level of involvement that their attentiveness towards other things or people minimizes and subverts their attention away from the things of God. In reference to church leaders, this often involves things that they should be doing in their capacity as church leaders.

In most cases, the distractions are comprised of things that legitimately fall within the scope of the person's normal responsibilities. The problem is not that he attends to such concerns; the problem is the inordinate level of distraction and the degree to which the person is pulled away from other responsibilities. The term *"other gods"* is often used in reference to responsibilities such as a person's spouse, children, possessions, employment, etc. It can be applied to anything that prevents a person from fulfilling his or her responsibilities unto God. Such reference does not suggest that the person abandon his responsibilities to his other legitimate obligations; it merely highlights the necessity of the effective management of his time and attention.

Church leadership does not require the leader to forsake the "sacred connectivity" of his or her spousal relationship; however, it is imperative that the "leader spouse" learns to incorporate some spousal duties into his or her functions as a church leader. I strongly suggest that leaders include their spouse as part of the leadership team. Again, to whatever degree possible, without violating protocol, in order to preserve spousal connectivity, the leader's spouse must be included in some leadership activities.

In equal fashion, church leadership does not require leaders to forsake the well-being of their children, or their parental involvement with their children. The "leader parent" must successfully learn how to balance the responsibilities of parenting with the responsibilities of church leadership. Again, I strongly recommend that leader parents manage their time effectively to minimize the cancellation of activities involving their child or children. When it is absolutely necessary to make cancellations, leaders must be swift to accommodate the child in a way that "makes up" for the necessary cancellations.

One of the unfortunate realities of life is that which was spoken of God to Adam, a church leader in conflict with his spousal position. After the fall in the Garden of Eden, God pronounced to Adam that *"in the sweat of thy face shalt thou eat bread"* (Gen. 3:19). Paul confirmed to the saints at Thessalonica *"that if any would not work, neither should he eat"* (2 Thess. 3:10).

In most cases, the necessity of the church leader's employment is an irrefutable factor of life. As such, except in the case of paid staff, church leaders are often required to perform the duties of church around the duties of work. Depending on their profession, availability may be time restricted, or limited to certain days of the week. Church leaders must learn to work within the context of their availability until things change. Intrinsic in that statement is the admonition to allow God to make the change rather than an impatient church leader initiating such change. It is imperative that church leaders learn to wait on God in situations where life's circumstances are restrictive of their ability to engage to the degree desired.

While this list of responsibilities could go on and on, I'd like to consider just one additional area where a leader's responsibility cannot be negated without casting a negative aspersion on his or her capacity as a church leader. That involves the commitment to the leader's home and other physical possessions. The Bible declares, *"For if a man cannot manage his own household, how can he take care of God's church?"* (1 Tim. 3:5 NLT). Managing the duties of church leadership and managing the affairs of home are not mutually exclusive; they must both take place with an equal diligence. My sincere advice to church leaders is: do not forsake your responsibilities as a church leader; while, at the same time, do not forsake the responsibilities of taking care of that which God has given you. Remember, he that is faithful over a few things will be master over many. Conversely, said Jesus, he that cannot be trusted in a few things, cannot be trusted in many things.

The ability to balance the responsibilities of church leadership, along with all else leaders are required by life to do, and the skills to manage time concurrently, are essential requirements of church leaders. To be good church leaders at the expense of being poor spouses, marginal parents, bad employees, or those who do not take proper care of their possessions is unacceptable. On the other hand, being good spouses, excellent parents, great employees, and those who take meticulous care of all that they have at the expense of fulfilling their duties as diligent church leaders is equally unacceptable.

Church leaders must not have other "gods"!

Do not forsake your responsibilities as a church leader; while, at the same time, do not forsake the responsibilities of taking care of that which God has given you.

Principle *19*

Church Leaders Must Have a Sound Mind

But let him ask in faith, nothing wavering. For he that wavereth is like a wave of the sea driven with the wind and tossed. For let not that man think that he shall receive any thing of the Lord. A double minded man is unstable in all his ways. —James 1:6–8

For God hath not given us the spirit of fear; but of power, and of love, and of a sound mind. —2 Timothy 1:7

Having grown up in a church environment where there was ongoing conflict between emotionalism and intellectualism, I found myself constantly working to find a balance between the two. Of course, the emotional aspect of the environment made me feel good, but the intellectual content helped me to think more clearly. I recall that as an early teenager, I had to make a conscious decision that since I could not successfully create a balance between those two worlds, I would simply utilize both to the fullest extent of my capacity. As a result, I became a person who is deeply moved by the feeling of his emotions, while at the same time, being extremely inquisitive about knowledge. Halfway through high school, I'd already read a great deal of the works of several noted philosophers. By the time I finished high school, I was highly conversant in the thoughts of the Socratic philosophers of ancient Greece: Socrates, Plato, and Aristotle. Considered by many to be the greatest Greek philosopher of all time, Socrates's work in the arena of Western philosophy influenced both Aristotle and Plato to the point that the three of them became known as the Socratic philosophers.

Philosophy is often described as a love for learning for learning's sake. I attribute my love for learning to a local church leader, who happened to have been my childhood neighbor. He became my greatest mentor during the early years of my church leadership experience. James Archie Johnson was pastor of a local church, along with being the general secretary of the national church in which I grew up. He later became bishop of our local diocese, and the presiding bishop of the organization. Our close relationship continued until his death in 2015. He was a church leader extraordinaire!

I raise this issue because it illustrates the fundamental connection between the mind and the trajectory of one's life. The mind has three basic functions: it shapes thoughts, it develops desires, and it contributes to feelings. The fact is that the mind is in control of all that is shown publicly to be the person that we are. From the functions of the mind, we can appear to be unstable if we vacillate back and forth with little to no consistency in the decision-making process, going from one conclusion to another. On the other hand, we can demonstrate the attributes of mental stability by displaying the soundness of mind that arises from reflective thought prior to settling on a decision. The former is often referred to as double-mindedness. The biblical equivalent to such double-mindedness is instability. The Apostle James reminded us: *"A double minded [leader] is unstable in all his ways."* In a world, unlike philosophy, where people are constantly searching for concrete answers, instability is an instant turn-off. As James relates, it is tantamount to *"a wave of the sea driven with the wind and tossed."* The instability of a double-minded leader often becomes a red flag to those who are sincere in their commitment to Christ.

Rational Bible-centered thinking is critical to the average member of the average church. Often, those who embrace the church do not come from an orderly, well-adjusted life. Quite the contrary, many church members were dreadfully disoriented when they accepted the call to discipleship. In many cases, it was their brokenness that made their hearts susceptible to the gospel. Did not Jesus say in Mark 2:17, *"They that are whole have no need of the physician, but they that are sick: I came not to call the righteous, but sinners to repentance"*? Not necessarily seeking salvation, such broken followers were in search of stability in an otherwise unstable existence. Jesus continued to illustrate why He came by saying, in John 10:10, *"I am come that they might have life, and that they might have it more abundantly."*

A life void of mental stability is schizophrenic! While schizophrenia is characterized by inconsistent or contradictory elements, so is double-mindedness! In the above referenced text, Jesus began by saying, *"The thief cometh not, but for to steal, and to kill, and to destroy"* (John 10:10). Instability is nothing less than a tool used by the "thief of life" to steal our stability. It is Satan's weapon of choice to kill the *"spirit of a sound mind,"* which is given to every person who opens his or her heart to accept Christ as Lord and Savior. Instability is the devil's method of destroying both leader and follower. It absolutely does not belong in the church, nor can it be resident in those who lead the church.

God's prescription against the malady of instability can be found in Romans 12:2, where Paul wrote, *"And be not conformed to this world: but be ye transformed by the renewing of your mind, that ye may prove what is that good, and acceptable, and perfect, will of God."*

It is one's conformity—our compliance with the norms, standards, and ways of the world; our behavior that is in accordance with socially accepted standards of the world; our loyalty to the practices of the world; our similarity in form and type; our agreement in character—it is that conformity with the world that aids the enemy in his attempt to steal, kill, and destroy. Paul's alternative to the danger of conformity is the transformation of the mind. By such transformation, a leader is able to *"prove what is that good, and acceptable, and perfect, will of God."*

Church leaders are then able to comply with the words of Paul to the Philippian church: *"Let this mind be in you, which was also in Christ Jesus"* (Phil. 2:5).

Church leaders must have a sound mind!

Principle 20

Church Leaders Must Maintain a Respectable Reputation

Choose a good reputation over great riches; being held in high esteem is better than silver or gold.
—Proverbs 22:1 (NLT)

A good reputation is more valuable than costly perfume.
—Ecclesiastes 7:1 (NLT)

We then, as workers together with him, beseech you also that ye receive not the grace of God in vain.... Giving no offence in any thing, that the ministry be not blamed: But in all things approving ourselves as the ministers of God....
—2 Corinthians 6:1, 3–4

Old adages and idioms that have become pearls of wisdom for those of us who are old enough to remember them, and who learned to appreciate their wisdom, have influenced our thinking over the years. A couple of such sayings are: "You can't teach an old dog new tricks"; and, "Old habits are hard to break"! While there is some truth to such old proverbs, those of us who are actively involved in the church are fully aware of an experience that can bestow upon mankind the innate ability to absolutely change his human characteristics, and, to some extent, his personality. That experience is the central message of the Christian church. It is the message of regeneration through the power of repentance and sanctification. After baptism and the infilling of the Holy Spirit, a person's life undergoes a phenomenal spiritual revision. Such revision can nullify many of the negative contributions of his past and bring him into a relationship with God that opens up a bright future where the damning condemnations of his old way of life are removed and replaced by a new mindset. Paul said to the members of the church at Rome, *"And be not conformed to this world: but be ye transformed by the renewing of your mind, that ye may prove what is that good, and acceptable, and perfect, will of God"* (Rom. 12:2).

While we cannot do anything about our "pre-salvation" reputation, a reputation earned during the many years spent living as servants of sin, our "post-salvation" experience will certainly put us in the position of carving out a new reputation that is reflective of the new lifestyle resulting from the experience of regeneration. At that point, the goal of earning a reputation that shows the effects of the Holy Spirit in operation in our life becomes integrated with our primary objective of pleasing God. As we walk with God, the evidence of our good reputation will become more and more pronounced! That which is needed to maintain such reputation is a continuation of that which was done to start the journey towards a good reputation.

Paul encouraged church leaders in the Corinthian church to live their lives in a way that would not bring negative blame upon the church. Rather, they are to live so that those around them can see them as leaders in the Lord's church. He said in 2 Corinthians 6:4–10:

Principle 20: Must Maintain a Respectable Reputation

But in all things approving ourselves as the ministers of God, in much patience, in afflictions, in necessities, in distresses, in stripes, in imprisonments, in tumults, in labours, in watchings, in fastings; by pureness, by knowledge, by longsuffering, by kindness, by the Holy Ghost, by love unfeigned, by the word of truth, by the power of God, by the armour of righteousness on the right hand and on the left, by honour and dishonour, by evil report and good report: as deceivers, and yet true; as unknown, and yet well known; as dying, and, behold, we live; as chastened, and not killed; as sorrowful, yet alway rejoicing; as poor, yet making many rich; as having nothing, and yet possessing all things.

It is essential that in all circumstances of life, both negative and positive, we conduct our affairs in a way that does not bring reproach upon the church. For to do otherwise will result in the dilution of the effectiveness of both our leadership within the church, and the church itself! This not only hurts the church leader, but it also heaps irreparable harm upon those served by their leadership. A prudent leader is sensitive to the reality that the followers are constantly being bombarded by the antics of Satan. The leader is aware that any additional negative examples of life emanating from his or her behavior, despite the cause, makes the followers' efforts even more difficult.

The value of a good reputation demonstrated in the life of church leaders can never be overstated. Such reputation gives credence to every decision made and every act of leadership performed. Church leaders must measure their activity against the yardstick of "cause and effect." In other words, they must ask of themselves, "How will this action be interpreted by my followers?" "Will my followers see this action in a manner that will build them up?" "Will their reaction to this decision hurt them or help them?" The responsibility of church leaders is to govern themselves in a manner that is beneficial to the development and spiritual growth of those within their charge.

A church leader's reputation is created by the actions and choices made over an extended period of time. Once made, such reputation, good, bad, or indifferent, will usually last over an even greater period. It will influence how others respond to his or her leadership. I assure you that a good reputation is easier to lose than it is to gain; once lost, it's very difficult to regain. My advice to every church leader is to earn the best reputation your mind can imagine. Once earned, do everything within your power to maintain what you have worked so hard to achieve. And for the record, that good reputation must exist among church members, and among those who are not a part of your church leadership experience.

Church leaders must maintain a respectable reputation!

Principle *21*

Church Leaders Must Be Spirit-Filled

Wherefore, brethren, look ye out among you seven men of honest report, full of the Holy Ghost and wisdom, whom we may appoint over this business. —Acts 6:3

The Book of Acts presents a plethora of examples of people being filled with the Holy Ghost, along with the positive results of their works. Yet, in today's church, somehow, we have accelerated the false premise that the work of the church can be done just as effectively by persons who have not experienced the infilling of the Holy Spirit, and that such status does not impede the work of the church. Quite the contrary! Even a casual reader will conclude after reading the narratives contained in the Book of Acts that there is a most definitive advantage to having those who will dare attempt to serve as leaders of the church to be first filled with the Holy Ghost.

I find it both interesting and suggestive how Apostle Luke, the writer of the Book of Acts, prefaced the narratives of the twenty-eight chapters that make up its context. He begins in verses 1–5 of chapter one:

> *The former treatise have I made, O Theophilus, of all that Jesus began both to do and teach, until the day*

in which he was taken up, after that he through the Holy Ghost had given commandments unto the apostles whom he had chosen: to whom also he shewed himself alive after his passion by many infallible proofs, being seen of them forty days, and speaking of the things pertaining to the kingdom of God: and, being assembled together with them, commanded them that they should not depart from Jerusalem, but wait for the promise of the Father, which, saith he, ye have heard of me. For John truly baptized with water; but ye shall be baptized with the Holy Ghost not many days hence. (Acts 1:1–5)

Halfway through verse 4, Luke quotes Jesus as saying,

Wait for the promise of the Father, which ye have heard of me. For John truly baptized with water; but ye shall be baptized with the Holy Ghost not many days hence.

The instructions are, in essence, "Do not leave Jerusalem to begin your work in ministry, until you have received the Holy Ghost."

Luke quotes Jesus again in verse 8, as saying, *"But ye shall receive power, after that the Holy Ghost is come upon you: and ye shall be witnesses unto me both in Jerusalem, and in all Judæa, and in Samaria, and unto the uttermost part of the earth."*

Luke's rendition of Jesus's statement speaks even more definitively in Luke 24:49: *"And, behold, I send the promise of my Father upon you: but tarry ye in the city of Jerusalem, until ye be endued with power from on high."*

The essence of verse 8 of Acts 1, and verse 49 of Luke 24, is that by waiting, they will be empowered to fulfill the purpose for which they were called. Any spirit-filled leader can attest that the Holy

Spirit does indeed provide for us the innate ability to perform the tasks necessary for the fulfillment of our God-given responsibilities in the church. This does not, however, suggest that leaders should not seek additional training in the areas of their leadership responsibilities. Nor does it suggest that the appointing leader is relieved of the responsibility to provide adequate supervision to those appointed into leadership positions within the church. And even though Luke alludes, in later renderings, to the reality that the Holy Spirit provides wisdom into which leaders can tap while performing the duties of their leadership roles, it remains incumbent upon both the appointed leader and the senior leader who makes such appointments to secure as much functional knowledge as possible for the impending responsibilities of leadership.

The infilling of the Holy Spirit is an indispensable part of any leader's preparation for leadership within the church. All necessary attributes for successful leadership can be accessed through compliance with the voice and directions of the Holy Spirit. It is this necessity of divine preparation that gives Acts 2 such lasting significance in the life of church leaders. This first cadre of one hundred twenty newly commissioned leaders of the New Testament church waited on the promise of Holy Spirit empowerment.

> *And when the day of Pentecost was fully come, they were all with one accord in one place. And suddenly there came a sound from heaven as of a rushing mighty wind, and it filled all the house where they were sitting. And there appeared unto them cloven tongues like as of fire, and it sat upon each of them. And they were all filled with the Holy Ghost.* (Acts 2:1–4)

I am not suggesting that with proper training, academic matriculation, leadership exposure, psychological maturity, and integrity of character, a person cannot evolve into an excellent leader within the context of any organization. I am, however, suggesting that if we are going to maximize our leadership potential within the Lord's church, it is imperative that leaders possess, along with each of the qualifying characteristics stated above, an infilling of the Holy Ghost equal to that of the leaders appointed by the apostles for the administration of the responsibilities of the early church in Acts 6:3:

> *Wherefore, brethren, look ye out among you seven men of honest report, full of the Holy Ghost and wisdom, whom we may appoint over this business.* (Acts 6:3)

Attempting to do God's work without the indwelling power of God is synonymous to trying to fly an airplane without the advantages of a vertical stabilizer and rudders, and a horizontal stabilizer and elevators without the benefit of pitch and yaw control. A plane can fly without a vertical stabilizer, but it would be very difficult for a human pilot to control yaw—the side-to-side movement of the nose of the aircraft. Unlike vertical stabilization, a plane cannot fly without a horizontal stabilizer; it would be impossible for a pilot to control pitch—the up and down movement of the aircraft nose. If a pilot wishes to fly with the least amount of destabilizing resistance in controlling the airplane, he will naturally opt for vertical and horizontal stabilizers. If a person wishes to lead the people of God in any leadership capacity, at any level, with the least amount of satanic or egomaniacal resistance, such person must seek God for the infilling of the Holy Ghost!

While these lessons deal primarily with church leaders and principles affecting such leaders, the tenants of this work are equally necessary for non-leader Christians who wish to enjoy a peaceful walk with God as they balance that walk with the distracting forces of life. The Holy Spirit is not only imperative for those who labor under the banner of church leadership, it is just as necessary for those whose life is void of any leadership responsibilities except in relationship to their own actions, and the activities of their concentric circle of contacts. The irony is that every one of us is a leader, if only in relationship to our own affairs! As one leads himself through the natural mazes of life, he needs the advantages of the Holy Spirit!

Church leaders must be Spirit-filled!

All necessary attributes for successful leadership can be accessed through compliance with the voice and directions of the Holy Spirit.

Principle 22

Church Leaders Must Be Dependable

If a man vows a vow to the Lord , or swears an oath to bind himself by a pledge, he shall not break his word. He shall do according to all that proceeds out of his mouth.
—Numbers 30:2

But whoever keeps his word, in him truly the love of God is perfected. By this we may know that we are in him: whoever says he abides in him ought to walk in the same way in which he walked. —1 John 2:5–6

I can recall reading, as a young man, a sign in the lobby of my local post office. I was told that although it was displayed in the postal building, it was not an official slogan. At the time I thought it should have been, but as time went on, I understood why it was not. It read:

> Neither snow, nor rain, nor heat, nor gloom of night stays these couriers from the swift completion of their appointed rounds.

I seem to recall a time when that slogan would have applied to postal workers throughout the country; however, in the ever-changing society of today, that once stable commodity has almost evaporated into a mere fragment of what it once was. In fact, in recent years, we have heard discussions of gross inconsistencies and inadequacies in our postal service. Any dependability in the delivery of mail that might have once been anticipated and enjoyed, has become more and more fragmented. Over the years, I have seen an extraordinary level of unpredictability in the services provided by our beloved postal service.

Whatever the cause, be it financial incapacity, the lack of human resources, or postal employees who just don't care anymore, a once dependable agency has become the face of unreliability. This can happen to any organization that fails to engage in prudent administrative practices. It could even happen to the church if its leaders are not conscientious and dependable. It is incumbent upon church leaders to hold in godly order the reputation and good standings of the church by being diligent in their responsibilities to God and to the office to which they are assigned. Anytime a leader in the church fails to maintain the dignity of his leadership duties, he diminishes ever so slightly the goodwill of the whole. It must be known that the success of any church is only as good as its reputation within the community. As such, the universal church can be negatively impacted as a whole by the bad faith actions of a few. (My use of the term "universal church" does not refer to the Catholic Church, but rather the church community altogether.)

The Bible is replete with the call of saints to live holy, to walk up right before the Lord, to walk worthy of their call, to not bring upon the church open shame: *"...seeing they crucify to themselves the Son of God afresh, and put him to an open shame"* (Heb. 6:6 ASV). The question is raised in one New Testament text: *"...of how much sorer punishment, suppose ye, shall he be thought worthy, who hath trodden under foot the Son of God, and hath counted the blood of the covenant, wherewith he was sanctified, an unholy thing, and hath done despite unto the Spirit of grace?"* (Heb. 10:29).

Indeed, those who are called into the church; those who by grace are brought to repentance; those whose sins are remitted by the sacred waters of baptism; those whose lives have been transformed by the indwelling of the Holy Spirit; indeed, such persons do carry the responsibility of holding sacred the church and its righteous standing. Paul can be heard urging the Colossians saints:

> *As therefore ye received Christ Jesus the Lord, so walk in him, rooted and builded up in him, and established in your faith, even as ye were taught, abounding in thanksgiving. Take heed lest there shall be any one that maketh spoil of you through his philosophy and vain deceit, after the tradition of men, after the rudiments of the world, and not after Christ: for in him dwelleth all the fulness of the Godhead bodily, and in him ye are made full, who is the head of all principality and power: in whom ye were also circumcised with a circumcision not made with hands, in the putting off of the body of the flesh, in the circumcision of Christ; having been buried with him in baptism, wherein ye were also raised with him through faith in the working of God, who raised him from the dead. And you, being dead through your trespasses and the uncircumcision of your flesh, you, I say, did he make alive together with him, having forgiven us all our trespasses; having blotted out the bond written in ordinances that was against us, which was contrary to us: and he hath taken it out of the way, nailing it to the cross....* (Colossians 2:6–14 ASV)

What an investment Christ made of Himself for our sakes, that we might become leaders in Him and leaders for His church. God granted to us the grace to hold in trust the good name of the Lord and the Lord's church. How then can we fail God's purpose in our sanctification? Church leaders must hold fast the reliability that God expects of us! The Chinese philosopher, Confucius, taught his followers: "A man who lacks reliability is utterly useless."

We must sing again the song of my youth, a song in which we petitioned the Lord, "Use me, Lord, in Thy service!" It seems as if I can hear the Lord responding by saying, "I want to use you; I want to use you in My service, but you must be dependable—you must be reliable!" Now comes the final question: Can the Lord use you? Will your leadership be dependable? Can the Lord rely on you? Can God really use you? That is the relevant question for church leaders!

Church leaders must be dependable!

Principle 23

Church Leaders Must Be Givers of Time and Substance

I must work the works of him that sent me, while it is day; the night cometh, when no man can work.

— John 9:4

So then, while we have opportunity, let us do good to all people, and especially to those who are of the household of the faith.   — Galatians 6:10

The work of a church leader does not start when he walks into the church, nor does it end when he leaves the church. Church leadership is an imposing position that penetrates every aspect of the leader's life and substance. Neither the leader's time nor substance belongs exclusively to him. The truth is that time and substance have never belonged to the individuals who utilized, or failed to utilize, them; rather, they have always belonged to God. The Bible teaches that: *"The earth is the LORD'S, and the fulness thereof; The world, and they that dwell therein"* (Psa. 24:1).

As such, all that a leader, or anyone else for that matter, has belongs wholly to God! The use of time and substance is on loan from God, who, in turn, monitors all activity stemming from such use. The narrative of the talents, as written in the synoptic gospels, which were distributed to the master's servants *"according to [their] several [abilities],"* illustrates the level of accountability to which God holds those appointed by Him to lead His church and His people.

> *For the kingdom of heaven is as a man travelling into a far country, who called his own servants, and delivered unto them his goods. And unto one he gave five talents, to another two, and to another one; to every man according to his several ability; and straightway took his journey.* (Matthew 25:14–15)

At some point, all people—including church leaders—will be held accountable for the use of time and substance given to them of the Lord. The narrative of Matthew 25 continues with this illustration of accountability in verses 16–27:

> *Then he that had received the five talents went and traded with the same, and made them other five talents. And likewise he that had received two, he also gained other two. But he that had received one went and digged in the earth, and hid his Lord's money. After a long time the Lord of those servants cometh, and reckoneth with them. And so he that had received five talents came and brought other five talents, saying, Lord, thou deliveredst unto me five talents: behold, I have gained beside them five talents more. His Lord said unto him, Well done, thou good and faithful servant: thou hast been faithful over a few things, I will make thee ruler over many things: enter thou into the joy of thy Lord. He also that had received two talents came and said, Lord, thou deliveredst unto me two talents: behold, I have gained two other talents beside them. His Lord said unto him, Well done, good and faithful servant; thou hast been*

faithful over a few things, I will make thee ruler over many things: enter thou into the joy of thy Lord. Then he which had received the one talent came and said, Lord, I knew thee that thou art an hard man, reaping where thou hast not sown, and gathering where thou hast not strawed: and I was afraid, and went and hid thy talent in the earth: lo, there thou hast that is thine. His Lord answered and said unto him, Thou wicked and slothful servant, thou knewest that I reap where I sowed not, and gather where I have not strawed: thou oughtest therefore to have put my money to the exchangers, and then at my coming I should have received mine own with usury.

God continues to call His servants, *"according to [their] several [abilities],"* into the service of the leadership of the various phases of His church and its affiliated operations, including local church, district, jurisdictional, diocese, national, or international operations. God's call into the leadership of His church also includes organizations and entities such as schools, seminaries, media outlets, etc., that support church and or religious functions. Leaders of all church related entities are to be governed by the same leadership principles as those who serve as leaders within the church itself. In terms of responsibility, all leaders within the church, or any support organization of the church, belong, by virtue of their leadership, to the position he or she holds. As such, leaders and all that we have, and all that we are belong to the service of the position we serve.

It is important to notice the phraseology used above, as was taken from Matthew's pericope: *"...according to [their] several [abilities]"*! A syntactical analysis of this phrase denotes that the number of talents assigned to each servant was in response to the master's own evaluation of each servant's capacities and capabilities. It is unfortunate that in today's church, often such evaluation of the capacity and capability of leaders is not factored into the assignment of leadership duties and responsibilities. Obviously, leaders cannot be expected to do what they are incapable of doing. Of course, there are exceptions, but the exceptions must be impressed upon the appointing leader by God.

This is confirmed by the Old Testament account of Moses's appointment to lead the children of Israel out of Egypt. The record shows that Moses suffered from a speech impediment, which would make it difficult for him to effectively communicate with both the people of Egypt and the children of Israel. God's appointment of Moses was proof-positive that the matter of Moses's handicap would not interfere with the performance of Moses's duties. I am delighted to have served the church long enough to have witnessed other such "leadership miracles"—whereby people who would seem to a casual observer to be incapable of the mental or physical rigors of leadership, but who were chosen by God for such task—excel in every responsibility involved with such leadership.

One final point I would like to impress upon those serving in leadership roles in the church is that such persons must not restrict their expenditures of time or resources to paid services or reimbursable purchases. Of course, reasonable churches are committed to holding leaders harmless when it comes to the minor acquisition of things such as supplies, equipment, and other expenses that are occasioned by the official responsibilities of such leaders, be they budgeted or non-budgeted expenses. By use of the term "reasonable churches," I am referring to churches that are led by prudent, well-balanced leaders.

However, I must caution all leaders to, as much as possible, consult with the leader to whom you are responsible prior to any expenses for which you wish to be reimbursed. In cases where leaders arbitrarily decide to enhance their event by providing convenience

Principle 23: Must Be Givers of Time and Substance

items such as gifts, paper, refreshments, decorations, mailings, etc., remember that it is better to give than to receive. Also, keep in mind that the God for whom you work has the best reimbursement program known to man! I cannot count the times I have gone into my pocket to financially facilitate my leadership responsibilities or activities; neither can I calculate the times when God has blessed me abundantly with financial resources beyond my wildest expectations.

Church leaders must be givers of time and substance!

If You Are Enjoying This Book, Will You Help Me Spread the Word?

There are several ways you can help me get the word out about the message of this book…

- Visit my website, and leave a review: 52principlesforchurchleaders.com

- Recommend the book to friends and fellow church leaders. Word of mouth is still the more effective form of advertising.

- Purchase additional copies to give away as gifts.

- Post a 5-Star review on Amazon, Goodreads and other places that come to mind.

- Write about the book on your Facebook, Twitter, Instagram, Google+, any social media sites you regularly use.

- Post a photo of yourself with the book on your social media.

- Ask bookstores if they carry the book. If not, they can easily order it through all major distributors.

- If you blog, consider referencing the book, or publishing an excerpt from the book with a link back to the website where you bought it.

- Do you know a podcaster, journalist or media personality who might be willing to interview me or write an article based on the book?

- Contact me by email at 52principlesbook@gmail.com.

Principle 24

Church Leaders Must Be Grounded in the Faith

Therefore, my beloved brethren, be ye stedfast, unmoveable, always abounding in the work of the Lord, forasmuch as ye know that your labour is not in vain in the Lord. —1 Corinthians 15:58

If ye continue in the faith grounded and settled, and be not moved away from the hope of the gospel, which ye have heard, and which was preached to every creature which is under heaven; whereof I Paul am made a minister. ... —Colossians 1:23

Of the many things expected of church leaders by both those *for whom* they are responsible and those *to whom* they are responsible, is a degree of steadfastness that is unparalleled by those outside of the ranks of leadership. If no other elements of leadership readiness are present in perspective church leaders, they should certainly be grounded in both their faith and their commitment to the church in which they serve. This is most essential because an unspoken element of a church leader's responsibility is that of assisting in the stabilization of those who make up the constituency of the church. Not only do church leaders serve as a calming force during times of difficulties for the church or its members, but in addition, effective church leaders serve as reinforcement agents for the teaching of the church. Stable leaders serve as valuable representatives of the church and the God of the church in affirming such matters pertaining to the doctrine of the church, and the teaching of the Bible.

Of course, this assumes that church leaders subscribe to the admonition given by Apostle Paul to the church as stated in 1 Corinthians 15:58. Here Paul urges the leaders of the church, whom he refers to as his beloved brethren, to *"be ye stedfast, unmoveable, always abounding in the work of the Lord, forasmuch as ye know that your labour is not in vain in the Lord."* Paul understood that by the time saints reach the level where their faith has matured enough to be placed into leadership positions in the church, they have made the necessary commitments as to the alignment of their faith practices with biblical principles, and in the relationship of their work with the promises of God. Such leaders understand the need for an affirmation of the faithful performance of the duties assigned to their hands. Paul parallels the responsibility of a leader's work with the knowledge that such leader is instinctively aware that his labor is not in vain in the Lord. As many pastors are forced to address all too often, one of the challenges a leader faces is that of assuring congregants that the services they provide to the Lord, by way of their labor in the Lord's church, do not go unnoticed. This, obviously, coincides with the need of all humanity to feel valued and appreciated for the contributions they make to the group in which they are involved.

Based upon such knowledge, Paul encourages the leaders at Corinth to be steadfast, to be unmovable, and to position themselves so that they are constantly abounding in the work of the Lord. He is suggesting that because leaders know that their labor is not in vain, they can be firm in their belief, their determination, and their adherence to both their faith commitment and their leadership commitment. Paul's use of the term *"unmovable"* denotes that such leaders are firmly fixed in place; such leaders work in a way that demonstrate that there is no possibility that they will change their relationship to the work to which they have been called. The church leaders described by Paul find themselves pressing to exceed that which is nominally expected of them. Such leaders are not satisfied with merely meeting the demands of the task set before them. They work with a determination to go above and beyond any minimum standard that has been ascribed to the position.

Leaders will never enjoy the satisfaction of being great leaders if they are content with merely doing what is expected. Successful leadership requires the establishment of goals that reflect a work ethic that supersedes accepted norms. Jesus alludes to this idea of "excellence beyond normality" in His discussion with His disciples on their state of righteousness during what we refer to as the "Sermon on the Mount." In verse 20 of Matthew 5, Jesus says, *"For I say unto you, That except your righteousness shall exceed the righteousness of the scribes and Pharisees, ye shall in no case enter into the kingdom of heaven."*

While I am aware that the narrative of this twenty-fourth principle does in no way speak to the hypocritical posture of those scribes and Pharisees referenced by Jesus, it is important to note that in today's church, we must contend with those whose state of self-righteousness places them in the same mental posture as that possessed by the scribes and Pharisees. Unfortunately, our churches are riddled with pharisaic personalities, who often hold themselves above the reach of appointed or elected leaders. Somehow, they feel as if they can only be instructed by God Himself. Please note, dear church leaders, when, having been duly chosen by God, you walk in harmony with God's Word and those leaders above you, then you can indeed speak with the authority of God. While I can assure you that you will, from time to time, encounter such behavior, often from persons from whom it is least expected, I encourage you not to allow such behavior to throw you off balance. I urge you to continue with the same steadfastness, the same immovability, and at the same degree of abounding in the work of the Lord to which you, as a sincere church leader, are committed. I further encourage you, as did Paul to the Colossian church, to *"continue in the faith grounded and settled, and be not moved away from the hope of the gospel"* (Col. 1:23).

Church leaders must be grounded in the faith!

Principle 25

Church Leaders Must Practice Honesty

Therefore seeing we have this ministry, as we have received mercy, we faint not; but have renounced the hidden things of dishonesty, not walking in craftiness, nor handling the word of God deceitfully; but by manifestation of the truth commending ourselves to every man's conscience in the sight of God. —2 Corinthians 4:1–2

The only honest definition of "honesty" is "the quality of being honest"! The only honest definition for "being honest" is to be truthful and free of deceit in all things. At first glance, that statement might sound like doublespeak; however, it is not at all. Let me explain. Doublespeak is to speak in a way that is deliberately euphemistic, ambiguous, or obscure. Honestly, this is not doublespeak! Doublespeak is designed to deceive; it is not intended to clarify. Doublespeak is very much akin to lying. The problem with lying is not simply that it gives false information, but at its core, it seeks to deceive. Deception is the core ingredient in a lie. I have long taught that a lie consists of three factors that, when ignored, will rob us of any vestige of honesty.

First, a lie exists when a person says something, or acts in a way, that he knows to be untrue. Secondly, a lie exists when what is said or done, is intended to deceive. Thirdly, the perpetrator of such false information, or action, seeks to gain from his statement or action. Please note, such gain is not limited to monetary or economic gain. It could simply be the expectancy of better acceptance by the group with which one associates; it could be designed to enhance one's reputation, or it could be a gain in status or position. Any deceit from which a person expects to benefit becomes part of the construct of a lie. Lying, and the intent to deceive, are inseparable co-equals. We must be careful to distinguish between a lie and the mistake of false information that was innocently given in ignorance and was not intended to deceive. False information given unknowingly may not necessarily constitute a lie. The greatest culprit is the person's intent to deceive.

This is all very important for those who are engaged in the business of leadership within the context of the church. Its importance is due to the expectation that such person must practice honesty at its highest level. Honesty must always be viewed as the absence of deceit; that obviously includes the absence of the practice of lying. Church leaders must guard against the appearance of lying! As such, a church leader must not repeat anything that he has not been able to verify. An excellent rule of thumb for all leaders is to follow the biblical recommendation given by Jesus to Nicodemus: *"Verily, verily, I say unto thee, We speak that we do know, and testify that we have seen..."* (John 3:11).

The Bible speaks quite strongly against liars, because lying represents the following three forms of trickery: false statements or actions, deceit, and manipulation for self-gain. There is absolutely no trace of honesty in that recipe! Leaders whose statements or actions fall into the category of manipulation will not enjoy the honor of successful leadership.

> *Lying lips are abomination to the* Lord. (Proverbs 12:22)

These six things doth the LORD hate: Yea, seven are an abomination unto him: A proud look, a lying tongue ... A false witness that speaketh lies.... (Proverbs 6:16–17, 19)

...and all liars, shall have their part in the lake which burneth with fire and brimstone.... (Revelation 21:8)

Conscientious church leaders will conduct themselves in a manner that consistently demonstrates the character and virtue necessary to ensure a reputation of honesty in the day-to-day activities of life. Such leaders must concern themselves with the following six areas:

Practice Honesty with Yourself

A cardinal rule for church leaders is to be absolutely honest with yourself about yourself. Acknowledge any flaws or idiosyncratic quirks that are part of your personality. Any person who cannot, or will not, be honest with himself cannot be expected to be honest with anyone else. Leaders who lie to themselves will surely lie to others. Most often, the gain of lying to themselves is generally for the purpose of concealing a moral flaw that they cannot otherwise deal with. When their thinking is so shallow that they can deceive themselves, they will feel no compunction about their efforts to deceive others. I need not suggest that those who actively suffer from such psychosis are not the most appropriate candidates for leadership and should not be appointed to the leadership team of a church, or church related entity, without strict supervision and accountability.

Practice Honesty with God

There is an adage that suggests that one can fool some of the people some of the time, but one cannot fool God any of the time. Psalm

139 is an in-depth acknowledgment of God's complete awareness of His human subjects. The psalmist begins by saying:

> *You have searched me, Lord, and you know me. You know when I sit and when I rise; you perceive my thoughts from afar. You discern my going out and my lying down; you are familiar with all my ways. Before a word is on my tongue you, Lord, know it completely.* (Psalm 1–4 NIV)

The psalmist then acknowledges that no matter where he goes or what he does, he cannot escape God's knowledge of him or his whereabouts (see Psalm 7–12 NIV). He continues:

> *My frame was not hidden from you when I was made in the secret place, when I was woven together in the depths of the earth. Your eyes saw my unformed body; all the days ordained for me were written in your book before one of them came to be.* (Psalm 15–16 NIV)

The wisest thing church leaders can do in relationship to God's awareness of the intricacies of their personalities is to turn pleadingly to God for help in making the necessary adjustments so that they can be used of God. To seek to conceal their flaws, or to do anything else designed to deceive God, would be a foolish attempt in absurdity!

Practice Honesty with Senior Leaders

It would do all church leaders well to acknowledge that senior leaders must give an account for those charged into their care. Just as you are responsible for those charged into your care, senior leaders are responsible for those charged into their care. They do not wish to see you fail; their sincere desire is for you to succeed in the work of the Lord. To put it mildly, your success is linked to theirs; conversely, your failure is, in part, their failure. Senior leaders do well when those charged to them do well! Again, the converse of that is also true. God, in His divine providence, designed it that way.

> *Obey them that have the rule over you, and submit yourselves: for they watch for your souls, as they that must give account, that they may do it with joy, and not with grief: for that is unprofitable for you.* (Hebrews 13:17)

Practice Honesty with Your Church

One of the most frequent complaints I hear from senior leaders, especially within the local church context, is that of church leaders accepting a less desired position with the intent of merely building a "steppingstone" to a more desirable position of a higher status. A steppingstone is regarded as a position or event that one engages in for the sole purpose of helping such person make progress towards pursuing what is believed by such person to be a loftier position or status. Please adhere to this alert: "If you are not going to serve the position for the position's sake, please do not accept the position." You may get away with that action a few times, but eventually, it will come back to haunt you. To accept a position to which you do not intend to commit is an act of deceit; it deceives the appointing leader into thinking you are interested in, and committed to, a position when you know you are not. Again, it's a deceitful lie!

This does not suggest that you cannot "climb the leadership ladder!" Indeed, you can, and should, climb as high as your skills, personality, and spirituality allows. However, each position in which you serve is entitled to your full attention and commitment. If you know, going into a position, that you are not going to serve the position honestly, please do not accept the position. To do so may cause unnecessary hurt to those affected by your callous disregard.

Practice Honesty with Your Household

As church leaders must know and practice honesty with themselves, the same level of honesty must be practiced towards those with whom they reside. Sociologists warn that those who most often suffer the brunt of one's anxiety are those who are closest to such person. Since those who live with you are intrinsically doomed to suffer the greatest consequence, the courtesy of honesty is highly suggested. To do otherwise would be disrespectful and non-Christian.

Practice Honesty with Your Followers

To successfully serve those assigned to any leader, there must be a modicum of respect and reverence that flows freely from the follower to the leader. Reverence speaks of respect based upon one's position, respect that is earned by ability, qualities, or achievements. If followers are to respect their leaders, the leaders must practice a level of honesty that warrants such respect. A standing rule of thumb in the practice of honesty is: "Never lie to your followers; and never, never seek to deceive followers!" An additional rule that I have practiced and taught over the past three decades is: "Never take advantage of followers for the purpose of aggrandizing yourself!" This includes, but is not limited to, economic, social, political, or any other action wherein a leader seeks to increase his power, status, or wealth; or whereby such leader seeks to enhance his reputation beyond what is justified by the position he holds.

A Final Note on the Practice of Honesty

While speaking about those who would seek to do him harm, David prayed, *"Deliver my soul, O Lord, from lying lips, and from a deceitful tongue"* (Psa. 120:2). I suggest, however, that this might be a prayer for church leaders to pray in the first person. It would look something like this: *"Deliver my soul, O Lord, from [my] lying lips, and from [my] deceitful tongue."*

An answer to such prayer could assist leaders tremendously in their quest to become the best church leader he or she is capable of becoming. Such status could prove to be of great benefit to both the church, and to the members thereof.

Church leaders must practice honesty!

*Conscientious church leaders
will conduct themselves in
a manner that consistently
demonstrates the character and
virtue necessary to ensure a
reputation of honesty in the
day-to-day activities of life.*

Principle 26

Church Leaders Must Maintain a Stable Family Life

Husbands, love your wives, even as Christ also loved the church, and gave himself for it.... So ought men to love their wives as their own bodies. He that loveth his wife loveth himself.... Nevertheless, let every one of you in particular so love his wife even as himself; and the wife see that she reverence her husband.
—Ephesians 5:25, 28, 33

Wives, submit yourselves unto your own husbands, as unto the Lord. For the husband is the head of the wife, even as Christ is the head of the church: and he is the saviour of the body. Therefore as the church is subject unto Christ, so let the wives be to their own husbands in every thing.   —Ephesians 5:22–24

Children, obey your parents in the Lord: for this is right. Honour thy father and mother; which is the first commandment with promise; that it may be well with thee, and thou mayest live long on the earth. And, ye fathers, provoke not your children to wrath: but bring them up in the nurture and admonition of the Lord.
—Ephesians 6:1–4

In a plethora of ways, life today is like Charles Dickens's novel, *A Tale of Two Cities,* which tells an intriguing story of two connected families in two of the world's most romantic cities, London and Paris, during the eighteenth century. Dickens's story touches on history, ethics, and the complexity of human relationships. The story begins with what has become one of the most famous lines in literature:

> It was the best of times, it was the worst of times, it was the age of foolishness, it was the epoch of belief, it was the epoch of incredulity, it was the season of Light, it was the season of Darkness, it was the spring of hope, it was the winter of despair, we had everything before us, we had nothing before us, we were all going direct to heaven, we were all going direct the other way....[4]

Like *A Tale of Two Cities*, these are the simplest of times; these are the most complex of times. In its simplest form, family is made up of a mother, a father, and in some cases, one or more offspring, who together form the nuclear family. Such family is a self-contained unit that is entitled to define its existence in the way that best suits its circumstances. It can be as private as it wishes, or it can be as transparent as it wishes; such decisions are left up to the family. In its most complex form, anything that anyone wishes to refer to as a family is acceptable to some elements of today's society. Those who dare to disagree with the gender makeup of some "so-called families," are often forced, by law, to accept them with the same grace with which one accepts the original concept of family. Such so-called families can be made up of two parenting partners that consist of two members of the same gender or could consist of an offspring whose gender identification has been transformed into the opposite gender. To any degree to which these families have

---

4   Dickens, C., (1859). *A Tale of Two Cities*. Chapman & Hall

been altered, they are still entitled to the same privileges of any other family. Life is indeed a tale of two families!

And, while privacy is the right of any family unit, the rapid transitions of lifestyle have negated most rights to privacy. This is especially true when it comes to members of the church. There exists an element outside of the church that wishes to discredit the church by any means possible. In pursuit of such goal, the anti-church elements of life are quick to expose the private concerns of any element of the church and the families who operate therein. Of course, in accordance with the teaching of evangelical theologians, of which I am one, the anti-church operatives have been functional since the prophecy of the Garden of Eden:

> *And the* Lord *God said unto the serpent, Because thou hast done this, thou art cursed above all cattle, and above every beast of the field; upon thy belly shalt thou go, and dust shalt thou eat all the days of thy life: and I will put enmity between thee and the woman, and between thy seed and her seed; it shall bruise thy head, and thou shalt bruise his heel.* (Genesis 3:14–15)

Evangelical theologians have long taught that the serpent was a prototype and symbol of Satan himself, while the seed of the woman represents Jesus Christ. As such, the prophecy contained in the Genesis text speaks to the ultimate battle between the things of Satan and the things which pertain to Christ. The church is, of course, Christ's most precious commodity; it is referred to in Scripture as the bride of Christ. Satan's desire to destroy the Lord's church is expressive of his desire to destroy the Lord. However, we also teach that the church is the offensive device of the Lord's strategies to bring salvation to all the world. Of such, Jesus said, *"And I say also unto thee ... I will build my church; and the gates of hell shall not prevail against it"* (Matt. 16:18).

In Satan's attempt to defeat Christ, he has waged an aggressive battle against the church by attacking the families of the church. For this reason, those called into the ministry of church leadership must be ever vigilant in their defense of the family unit. Church leaders must preserve and protect the family unit as it has been instituted by God. The family unit *must* consist of a male husband, a female wife, and children who are identified by the gender into which they were born. Please accept my three included suggestions for fathers, mothers, and children for protecting and preserving the family unit. The following suggestions are foundational, and do not represent every functional detail for the behavior of parents or offspring; they do provide the basic framework for the development of a stable family experience for church leaders.

Fathers

A father must demonstrate love for his wife and/or children. Such demonstration of love must be consistently shown by the father's actions and attitude; it must never become a tool of punishment whereby it is withheld during times of anger or dissatisfaction but shown during times of happiness and satisfaction.

A father must assume the position as head of the family. Headship does not merely speak to one's authority over another; but rather, it also speaks to one's responsibility to provide for and care for another. Such provision and care must include one's wife and all children born to, or brought into, that family unit. Headship does not negate the right of a wife to give input or to question any initiative affecting the family.

A father must set the tone for the development and behavior of the children in the home. The three objectives of such development are to prepare them for a lifelong relationship with God; to prepare them to live as productive adults with the innate ability to fulfill all responsibilities of adulthood; and prepare them to embrace this, and the above-mentioned functions of parenthood, as they mature into spouses and/or parents.

Mothers

A mother must be willing to follow the leadership of a prudent husband regarding daily family life. In doing so, mothers must be willing to give comments and offer suggestions for the purpose of providing additional insight in decisions affecting the home. Such willingness to follow and contribute insight must not be accompanied with anger, hostility, or harsh words.

A mother must show support and cooperation to her husband in his role of leader of the home. Mothers must insist that the children of the home are respectful and cooperative to both mother and father. She is to reinforce the husband in the development of the children.

A mother must be willing to manage the day-to-day details of the home regarding cleanliness, order, services, and hospitality. To manage is not to suggest that the mother must actually perform all housekeeping chores; it simply suggests that she exercises oversight as she, the husband, and children do their share as well.

Children

The cardinal rule for children in the home is that they obey their parents. The greatest desire for a parent is that their children excel in life and grow to become successful in whatever endeavor they pursue in life. Saved parents wish for their children that they have a lifelong relationship with God; that they live as productive adults with the ability to fulfill all responsibilities of adulthood; and that, when the time comes, they are prepared to perform the functions of parents as they become fathers and mothers.

By adhering to the above stated principles, a family will be stable and well-rounded as they grow in the work of the Lord. Please remember that when a mother or father is called to the position of church leadership, it automatically engages every member of the family. They, too, must adhere to the rules and principles of church leadership.

Church leaders must maintain a stable family life!

Principle 27

Church Leaders Must Be Humble

Humble yourselves therefore under the mighty hand of God, that he may exalt you in due time. —1 Peter 5:6

Humility is a recurring theme throughout the Bible. Almost every biblical writer either spoke about humility or was reminded to be humble. In some instances, they admonished others to be humble. It appears that humility might be a serious prerequisite for placement in the work of the Lord. I suggest that it is not merely an appearance, but a functional reality.

The first advantage of humility is that it demonstrates our awareness of God's hand in the blessings bestowed upon our lives. It speaks to the acknowledgment of a higher power in the affairs of our life; humility actually glorifies God. This is seen when we realize our inability to initiate the blessings of life through self-generated activity. This realization brings about an appreciation of God's grace and the resultant mercy that facilitates such blessings. It reminds us that we are forever indebted to God. Humility places us in subjection to God; it demonstrates our great dependence on the power of God, a power that is far greater than the combined strength of all humanity.

The second advantage of humility in the life of leaders is that it stops us from acting with an air of independence that may be perceived as arrogance or narcissism, first cousins that each depict their own negative nuance. Arrogance shows an inflated opinion of one's own importance, associated with what one thinks he can do. It gives rise to presumptive self-confidence, along with an attitude of superiority over others without regard to one's lack of achievements or the accomplishments of others. Narcissism speaks to one's excessive admiration of self; it is often seated in how one thinks he looks. While arrogance and narcissism border on egocentricity, sincere humility neutralizes both. It must be noted that humility is not a "one act at a time" situation; rather, in its most sincere form, humility becomes one's way of life. It permeates every aspect of one's life.

Paul speaks of humility in relationship to Jesus in his letter of Philippians 2:5–8:

> *Let this mind be in you, which was also in Christ Jesus: who, being in the form of God, thought it not robbery to be equal with God: but made himself of no reputation, and took upon him the form of a servant, and was made in the likeness of men: and being found in fashion as a man, he humbled himself, and became obedient unto death, even the death of the cross.*

We cannot detach the characteristics of humility from the earthly image of Jesus. For those who wish to reflect the image of Christ, they must do so in a spirit of humility. As Jesus, who *"thought it not robbery to be equal with God ... took upon him the form of a servant,"* we, too, as servant leaders in the Lord's church, must humble ourselves and become obedient unto the form of a servant. No leader can lead except in the form of a servant. Leaders must humble themselves to commit to serving those whom they lead. Of course, the margin of acceptability may be more lenient when it comes to business, civic, educational, or political leaders. It is unquestionably essential for church leaders to develop and maintain a posture of humility. This glorifies God as it acknowledges His sovereign power over the church, and those who labor in the church.

The importance of such attitude is undeniable; it illustrates one's deference to God! In addition to the necessity of our humble submission to, and respect for God, such deference places us in the position of being exalted by God. This is Peter's point in the text of this lesson: *"Humble yourselves therefore under the mighty hand of God, that he may exalt you in due time."*

An indispensable effect of humility in church leaders is that it fosters a level of patience that is intrinsic in humility. Peter's use of the phrase, *"in due time,"* at the end of the verse was not for grammatical or syntactical purposes; it was necessary to illustrate the pattern by which God works. God does not elevate us before we are spiritually, socially, psychologically, and egoistically ready. Please understand that our readiness is directly commensurate with our level of humility before God. Elevation is inextricably tied to humility! To my "wanna be slick" friends who traffic in dishonesty and deception, we cannot fake readiness; an attempt to do so simply confirms our lack of humility and unreadiness. The phrase, *"Be not deceived; God is not mocked,"* can be interpreted to say, "Don't play with God!"

To some church leaders, the connection between humility and the capacity for service may not be viewed with the required level of appreciation. However, to those who are sincere enough, and committed to God and the service of God enough to grasp the connection, humility will never be an issue. As humility is a prerequisite for leadership in the church, the lack of humility does grave damage to both the leader and the church. God may often appear silent in the face of such abomination; however, in due time, God will rise up against those who commit such injury upon His church. I can hear the words of Jeremiah screaming out God's warning to the leaders who wreaked havoc upon His people:

> *You leaders of my people are like shepherds that kill and scatter the sheep. You were supposed to take care of my people, but instead you chased them away. So now I'll punish you severely and make you pay for your crimes!... I promise to choose leaders who will care for them like real shepherds. All of my people will be there, and they will never again be frightened.* (Jeremiah 23:1–2, 4 CEV)

Church leaders who conscientiously go about the business of caring for the people of God in the context of the leadership charge placed upon them will reap great honor from God and the people of God. During the sixty years I have served the church, I have seen inexplicable blessings bestowed upon those who served with humility. Leaders who might seem unassuming, but who go about their labor with a dedication that shows their commitment to God and His people, were exalted to levels that can only be explained by the psalmist as the Lord's doing: *"This is the LORD's doing; It is marvellous in our eyes"* (Psa. 118:23).

Church leaders must be humble!

Principle 28

Church Leaders Must Know When to Hold 'em

To every thing there is a season, and a time to every purpose under the heaven: a time to be born, and a time to die; a time to plant, and a time to pluck up that which is planted; a time to kill, and a time to heal; a time to break down, and a time to build up; a time to weep, and a time to laugh; a time to mourn, and a time to dance; a time to cast away stones, and a time to gather stones together; a time to embrace, and a time to refrain from embracing; a time to get, and a time to lose; a time to keep, and a time to cast away; a time to rend, and a time to sew; a time to keep silence, and a time to speak; a time to love, and a time to hate; a time of war, and a time of peace.

—Ecclesiastes 3:1–8

The above text makes it very clear that timing is essential to all activities of life. Nowhere else in Scripture does a text go through such lengths to emphasize the importance of being certain that what we do is in tune with the appropriate timing. In verse 9 (not included above), the writer raises a concluding question: *"What profit hath he that worketh in that wherein he laboureth?"* Implicit in that question is the reality that our success in any endeavor is intricately connected with our ability to work in synchronization with the right timing.

The title of this lesson is taken from a song written by Donald Alan Schlitz Jr., a country music songwriter. As an example of the impact of the right timing, Schlitz struggled for a couple of years before writing "The Gambler" in 1976. He was working the graveyard shift as a computer operator when he was inspired to write the song that would change his life and earn a place in pop culture. In sync with the appropriate timing, Schlitz earned two Grammys and four ASCAP Country Songwriter of the Year awards. He was inducted into the Nashville Songwriters Hall of Fame.

The phrase, *"Know when to hold 'em,"* is a poker slang that refers to knowing when one's cards are good enough to play and when one should drop out of the game. *"You've got to know when to hold 'em; know when to fold 'em; know when to walk away; and know when to run"* is a line from the "The Gambler" as sang by Kenny Rogers.[5] The line refers to the strategy of knowing when to stay in a game and when to leave. It is often used as a metaphor suggestive of one's handling of life decisions—knowing when to persist and when to give up. It is a strategy that every church leader would benefit from knowing and practicing in his daily implementation of responsibilities. It could save us from having to contend with a great deal of the anxiety that often accompanies the functions of a church leader.

There are times when it is in the best interest of a leader to hold 'em; then, there are other times when it is in his best interest to fold 'em. Any prudent leader must differentiate between those circumstances and determine the appropriate actions. Church leadership is

---

5   Schlitz, D. A., (1976). *The gambler*. United Artists

not a "one size fits all" situation; but rather, it is one that requires vigilant observation and minute-by-minute flexibility.

Another line that I find quite beneficial in the fulfillment of one's functions as a church leader is: *"Son, I've made a life out of readin' people's faces, knowin' what the cards were by the way they held their eyes...."* Inasmuch as the church leader is often the intermediary between the body of members and senior leadership, it is imperative that they also serve as barometers for gauging the interests and attitudes of the members. By doing so, important matters can be addressed by senior leaders before they reach crisis levels. This saves a tremendous amount of wear and tear on both leader and members. It also shows great concern for the well-being of such members. I recommend the reading of 1 Corinthians 12:4–10:

> *Now there are diversities of gifts, but the same Spirit. And there are differences of administrations, but the same Lord. And there are diversities of operations, but it is the same God which worketh all in all. But the manifestation of the Spirit is given to every man to profit withal. For to one is given by the Spirit the word of wisdom; to another the word of knowledge by the same Spirit; to another faith by the same Spirit; to another the gifts of healing by the same Spirit; to another the working of miracles; to another prophecy; to another discerning of spirits; to another divers kinds of tongues; to another the interpretation of tongues....*

Another line that offers sage advice is: *"The secret to survivin' is knowin' what to throw away and knowin' what to keep."* It is not uncommon for church leaders at an intermediate level to find themselves involved with matters of such urgency that they can be better served by a higher level of leadership. Likewise, there are matters that do not reach that level of urgency. It is incumbent upon leaders to make the determination as accurately as possible. He must know what to throw away, and what to keep. The inherent risk of not referring weightier matters to a higher-level leader is that they could blow up and cause a major disturbance that could have been better contained at a "safer" stage. A residual risk is the loss of credibility for leaders who fail to make a reasonably accurate determination of such matters.

A final area of discussion from the song is: *"Cause every hand's a winner, and every hand's a loser."* Here, the implication is that the question of the success or failure of one's leadership experience is intrinsically hinged on the decisions and actions of each leader. Some leaders are certainly more gifted than others; but being gifted does not always result in leadership success. Natural giftedness can only prove beneficial when paired with the other necessary leadership principles. Another factor that might determine one's success or failure in leadership is the leader's ability to manage personality manifestations like arrogance, pride, temper, impatience, etc. An excessive presence of any of these will almost always result in immediate failure!

> *You've got to know when to hold 'em; know when to fold 'em; know when to walk away; and know when to run.*

Church leaders must know when to hold 'em!

Principle 29

Church Leaders Must Demonstrate a Measure of Faith

For I say, through the grace given unto me, to every man that is among you, not to think of himself more highly than he ought to think; but to think soberly, according as God hath dealt to every man the measure of faith.

—Romans 12:3

The Bible explicitly declares that without faith it is impossible to please God! Pleasing God must be the ultimate desire of all church leaders. There are many aspects of life that cannot be successfully navigated without the integration of faith. We know that faith is primarily associated with our interactions with God, but a measure of faith *must* be utilized if we expect to get along successfully with life, from a religious and non-religious perspective. To put it bluntly, life requires faith!

I have discovered during the past sixty years that the more abundant is our faith, then the more abundant is our ability to live an enjoyable life. I contend that an enjoyable life is one not plagued with the disruptions of constant anxiety, fear, and mental anguish. It is not necessarily money-based. I am not suggesting that money is not a commodity that we might find essential to a quality life; but money must not be viewed as the main ingredient of an enjoyable life. Instead, we must appreciate the undeniable fact that for those who live by the tenants of Christianity, an enjoyable life is tied intrinsically to the giver of life. We read in Ecclesiastes 6:2 (CEB):

> *God may give some people plenty of wealth, riches, and glory so that they lack nothing they desire. But God doesn't enable them to enjoy it; instead, a stranger enjoys it. This is pointless and a sickening tragedy.*

While my focus here is church leadership, any church member who expects to engage in a successful church experience must also develop some measure of faith. Too often, the average church member draws faith expectations from those who serve in leadership positions in the local church. Indeed, there are a plethora of reasons why faith is necessary among church leaders; however, in the absence of any other compelling reason, the following reason should be sufficient to bring about the transformation of faith from that of an average church member to that of a responsible church leader: church leaders must serve as "faith models" for the rest of the church membership! If those called into church leadership are to find success in their leadership responsibilities, at some point along the road to leadership, a transformation of faith must happen.

Because of the vital role faith plays in the life of members, it is important that leaders examine themselves in respect to their faith relationship with God! Ideally, this should be done prior to the appointment into church leadership. However, when administrative necessity causes us to be hurried into leadership, an assessment of the leader's faith must be an urgent priority if the leader is to enjoy the fruit of good leadership. When the spiritual survival of others depends on the examples of designated leaders, it is important that the leaders grasp the gravity of the assignment into which they have embarked. Leaders must be aware that what they do will negatively or positively influence those whom they have been designated to lead. In leadership, there is no middle ground, no neutrality; leaders either influence their followers positively, or cripple them with negativity. Thus, the importance of some measure of faith!

This is not to suggest an absence of faith; rather, my only objective is to emphasize the importance of the capacity of all leaders to demonstrate their reliance on God in the administration of their duties as leaders. My son recently shared a sermon during which he talked about three types of faith. He talked about a "receiving faith" as being our confidence that we will receive from God that which He promises. I must point out that inclusive in that promise is God's ability to guide us through the difficult moments of our work for Him. The second type of faith is a confidence in the fact that God will be with us and lead us as we live out our purpose in Him. And, finally, the faith that all of us must rely on daily is the confidence that God will sustain our righteousness and our commitment thereto.

Apostle Paul emphasized the effect of faith in God's ability to sustain the work that has been charged to our hands. Paul declared in Philippians 4:13, *"I can do all things through Christ which strengtheneth me."*

Paul is assuring us that God provides us with strength sufficient for the task to which He has charged us. God will never call us into a service that He does not strengthen us to do. Why, then, do so many church leaders fail to perform at an acceptable level? Of course, there are leaders who refuse to allow God to work in them the might necessary to carry out the duties assigned to them. The only thing we can say about leaders who refuse to yield to God's energizing strength, knowing that what they do is what sustains those dependent on their leadership, is that God will judge.

Also, there are those who stepped into leadership roles to which God did not call them! Consequently, performance of those responsibilities will not carry any commitment from God on behalf of such unsanctioned leaders, except to the degree that God responds to the needs of His people. I reiterate: when the call is of God, God's grace is always sufficient. It is appropriate to echo the words of God to Paul in reference to the difficulty Paul experienced in his ability to maintain sufficient health to carry out his God-ordained responsibilities. God said, *"My grace is sufficient for thee: for my strength is made perfect in weakness"* (2 Cor. 12:9).

Church leaders who cannot trust God will not experience the joy that comes when they maximize their potential in the Lord. The glory of God that attends such life is beyond any passion they can experience outside of God! Leaders must show in the conduct of the business of leadership a measure of faith as they lead the people of God!

Church leaders must demonstrate a measure of faith!

Principle *30*

Church Leaders Must Practice High Moral Values

Do not be deceived: "Bad company corrupts good morals." Be sober-minded [be sensible, wake up from your spiritual stupor] as you ought, and stop sinning; for some [of you] have no knowledge of God [you are disgracefully ignorant of Him, and ignore His truths]. I say this to your shame.
—1 Corinthians 15:33–34 (AMP)

At some point in our lives, we have all heard the term "moral compass"! Unfortunately, not all persons who hear the term are committed to its practice. Moral compass is a term used in reference to a person's ability to judge what is right and wrong and, as a result, act accordingly. We might ask the question: What contributes to one's moral compass? I submit that the moral compass is usually the result of several factors derived from a multitude of practices and interactions in a person's family and community. For churched families, a portion of what makes up the moral compass can be found in the doctrinal practices and spiritual beliefs of one's church. Other contributors to one's moral compass can be found in family values, cultural beliefs, social norms, and customs. When all is said and done, moral compass is all about our personal sense of morality.

Churches balanced in strong biblical teaching are excellent contributors to the development of a strong moral compass in those under their influence. Of course, such teaching must be displayed in the examples seen in the lives of the leaders and members if the churches are to make an impact that produces high levels of moral thinking and practices. Conversely, churches that approach biblical teaching from a "soft" perspective often become bastions of soft moral practices. We must be reminded that Paul's epistles were not written for sport. It was not simply a matter of Paul practicing his penmanship! Believe me, some letters were written in response to known negative behavior; some to highlight positive behavior as a method of preventing the initial occurrence of negative behavior. Such action often mitigated the development of bad moral practices.

In every human being lies the propensity for bad behavior and bad moral practices. Does not the Bible teach that we are shaped in iniquity and in sin did our mothers conceive us? Our ability for immorality and bad behavior is innate to humanity. Conversely, the ability to practice good morals must be acquired through an infusion of God consciousness and the association of good company. Apostle Paul made it clear to the saints at Corinth: *"Bad company corrupts good morals."* We can surmise from the context that negative behavior was already in practice. Paul continued by saying: *"Be sober-minded as you ought, and stop sinning...."*

My prior statement on the "infusion of God consciousness" is in respect to the infilling of the Holy Spirit! I've known people who, though not filled with the Holy Spirit, still practiced, over many years, good moral behavior in my presence. I can only assume that such persons were guided by a strong moral compass. Unfortunately, I cannot attest to their behavior when in bad company. I can say, however, that the presence of bad company can be a tremendous deterrent to good behavior. The absence of the Holy Spirit in one's life only makes the matter worse. Albeit, I must point out that the safest approach to good behavior is to experience the transforming power of the Holy Spirit, and to, as much as possible, abstain from bad company. I think it safe to assume that when Paul wrote to the church at Corinth, he was writing to Spirit-filled people!

One might ask: What is the advantage of a strong moral compass? Whether one is religious or not, one advantage is that having, and being guided by, such a moral compass will help us make better decisions. The practice of making good decisions always results in a better life. Another positive advantage is the ability to judge what is right and wrong and, as a result, act accordingly. This is echoed throughout Old and New Testament Scripture. Such examples can be found in Proverbs 11 (to cite a few):

A false balance is abomination to the LORD: But a just weight is his delight. (v. 1)

The integrity of the upright shall guide them: But the perverseness of transgressors shall destroy them. (v. 3)

The righteousness of the perfect shall direct his way: But the wicked shall fall by his own wickedness. (v. 5)

The righteousness of the upright shall deliver them: But transgressors shall be taken in their own naughtiness. (v. 6)

The righteous is delivered out of trouble, And the wicked cometh in his stead. (v. 8)

By the blessing of the upright the city is exalted: But it is overthrown by the mouth of the wicked. (v. 11)

> *As righteousness tendeth to life: So he that pursueth evil pursueth it to his own death.* (v. 19)

If a church, or church organization, is to develop members who enjoy the benefits of a strong moral compass, it must be a church where leaders practice and demonstrate such moral compass. While not practiced in some churches, I must insist that good leadership leads by example; such example must include moral integrity. An unknown source once said, "The glue that holds relationships together—including the relationship between the leader and the led—is trust, and trust is based on integrity."

The truth is that no matter how loudly one preaches virtue, his actions often drown out his shouting. The Reverend Harry Emerson Fosdick, the late pastor of the historic Riverside Church in Manhattan, New York, stated, "With many overhead schemes for the world's salvation, everything rests back on integrity and driving power in personal character." Leaders of today's church must be acutely aware of the necessity of strong personal character. Leaders must be equally aware that the development of such character is directly related to our moral compass. It is essential in the complex climate in which the church exists today, that church leaders understand that the church is not the place to play games with the eternal destiny of the souls of people. God will indeed judge those who passively or overtly cause harm to His dear children. If, for no other reason, church leaders at all levels of church leadership must possess the ability to command of their actions good behavior with the knowledge that what they do influences what others do.

Church leaders must practice high moral values!

Principle *31*

Church Leaders Must Know Who Jesus Is

When Jesus came into the coasts of Cæsarea Philippi, he asked his disciples, saying, Whom do men say that I the Son of man am? And they said, Some say that thou art John the Baptist: some, Elias; and others, Jeremias, or one of the prophets. He saith unto them, But whom say ye that I am? And Simon Peter answered and said, Thou art the Christ, the Son of the living God.

—Matthew 16:13–16

The primary focus of the Christian church, despite its denomination or branch, is Jesus. The church's purpose, selling point, and mission is to bring a lost and dying world into fellowship with Jesus Christ. While there are many other residual benefits of maintaining a relationship with Christ, one must never confuse benefits with the primary mission. Should that happen, intentionally or accidentally, it changes the trajectory of the church. Any change in the path of the church negatively affects the position of mankind to the church. The backbone of man's position with God is left in limbo. Humanity's pathway to salvation is shifted to a direction that ultimately leads to nowhere. This impairment misaligns man's relationship with the things of God. Eventually, and to the disadvantage of those whose hope lies in the eternal cohabitation with God, it threatens to change their basic attitude, beliefs, and feelings in relationship to the value of the church.

Despite the myriad of changes that have affected society since the advent of Christ, the church must remain focused on Jesus as the center of its reason for existing. Any hope of preserving that focus is intricately dependent upon the preservation of the knowledge of Christ by church leaders. They must know beyond any doubt who Jesus is! Intrinsically embodied in the word "who" is an understanding of the "what" and "why" of Jesus Christ.

The question raised by Jesus to His disciples in the text at the beginning of this lesson was more than a question to spark conversation or debate. The question was not the Lord's way of testing the disciples' ability to respond in a timely fashion, or even in an appropriate manner; the question was raised so that it could become part of the narrative of the Word of God. Throughout the years, this question has reminded the church that its focus must remain centered around the realization of who Jesus is.

Jesus was described by his forerunner, John the Baptist, as the Lamb of God, who takes away the sins of the world. John 1:29 states, *"The next day John seeth Jesus coming unto him, and saith, Behold the Lamb of God, which taketh away the sin of the world."*

Jesus was described by the Apostle Paul in 2 Corinthians 5:19, as the embodiment of God, reconciling the world unto himself: *"...to wit, that God was in Christ, reconciling the world unto himself, not imputing their trespasses unto them; and hath committed unto us the word of reconciliation."*

Jesus was also referenced as the propitiation for our sins: *"...and he is the propitiation for our sins: and not for ours only, but also for the sins of the whole world"* (1 John 2:2).

Principle 31: Must Know Who Jesus Is

The question Jesus raised was very deliberate; He asked succinctly: *"Whom do men say that I the Son of man am?"* After a plethora of different answers, Jesus, concluding that the people did not know who He was, became even more pointed in His questioning. This time, Jesus asked His newly appointed church leaders: *"But whom say ye that I am?"* The potency of that question is still relevant for today's church leaders. Its mere presence raises reflections that, when seriously considered, enhance our ability to produce the results intended by the question. It leads to the profound certainty that Jesus is the Christ, the Son of the living God.

When members of the church know unequivocally who Jesus is, that knowledge enhances the process of putting together the dismantled relationship of humanity to the church. It removes the relationship of mankind with God from the limbo of ignorance and disobedience. Mankind's pathway to salvation is then restored to its proper heading, leading to a revitalization of the things of God. It brings revival to the attitudes, beliefs, and feelings for the value of the church. The church is reacquainted with God! Jesus brings back into focus the mission of Christ, taking away the sins of the world, and reconciling the world back unto Himself; the actions of propitiating, or appeasing God, are all restored to the church.

When church leaders instinctively know the what, how, and why of Jesus, their ability to lead the people of God is exponentially increased to a level, and at a rate that not only can new members be added to the church daily, but current members will be reinforced in their relationship with Jesus to the extent that they will become enthusiastic about their worship and service to God and the church.

In Paul's discussions with the Galatian church, wherein he made some comparisons between their pre- and post-Christ relationships, he paralleled the idea of *"knowing God"* with *"being known of God."* He wrote, *"But now, after that ye have known God, or rath-*

er are known of God, how turn ye again to the weak and beggarly elements, whereunto ye desire again to be in bondage?" (Gal. 4:9).

While the benefit of knowing Jesus is in itself a blessing beyond comparison, it affords church leaders the ability to move through life with a sense of calm and comfort that places them in a peaceful position with life and its ever-changing circumstances. The security of living in the presence of Jesus, and being known of God, releases leaders from the anxieties that ordinarily push against their ability to serve the church without the apprehensions and secular concerns that often derail those whose relationship with Christ is marginal or nonexistent.

Church leaders must know who Jesus is!

Principle *32*

Church Leaders Must Not Be a Novice

The bishop therefore must be without reproach, the husband of one wife, temperate, sober-minded, orderly, given to hospitality, apt to teach; no brawler, no striker; but gentle, not contentious, no lover of money; one that ruleth well his own house, having his children in subjection with all gravity; (For if a man knoweth not how to rule his own house, how shall he take care of the church of God?) Not a novice, lest being lifted up with pride he fall into the condemnation of the devil. —1 Timothy 3:2–6

Approximately twenty minutes from where I live is a regionally famous racetrack where many of my neighbors and friends go to enjoy the horse races. Of course, some of them go to win a few extra bucks by betting on the horses. One of the terms I hear frequently from such friends is the word "novice." To my racehorse-betting colleagues, this word refers to a racehorse who has never won a serious race or received a major prize on the horse racing circuit. The idea is that such horse has not yet reached a level of performance which qualifies him for major events such as a horse race at Fairmont Park.

And, even though I was already familiar with the word, my familiarity was centered around a person classified as such within the context of the church. Having spent a great deal of time during my preteen and teenage years at Saint Rose Catholic School, located around the corner from my house, I had the privilege of talking with several nuns and priests who staffed the school. They, too, spoke of a novice, but in reference to what appeared to be a young nun or priest who was serving the religious order before taking their vows; such a person, referred to as a novice, was serving under probation.

Later, I became an avid student of Latin, of which I spent the next four years studying extensively. I learned that the word "novice" is derived from the Latin word *novus*, which means "new." The word evolved to mean a person who is inexperienced in or new to a particular situation, one who must be trained in his duties. Now, I am better able to understand Paul's instructions to Timothy as he instructed him on the role of a leader of the church. Paul cautioned Timothy that such person be *"not a novice, lest being puffed up he fall into the condemnation of the devil"* (1 Tim. 3:6).

Paul began his definition of a novice at the start of the conversation in verse 2. He said (in paraphrase): "Such leader must be old enough to have lived a life without reproach (in such a way that his contemporaries would not feel the need to express disapproval or disappointment)." Paul goes on to say (in paraphrase) that "such leader must be old enough and mentally stable enough to have selected a wife out of the many females he may have been involved with during his youth." Of course, this does not suggest that there are not leadership positions in the church that might be conducive to single persons, or that there are no situations where being single would be non-problematic.

The next five elements that certify a leader's non-novice status are: temperate, sober-minded, orderly, given to hospitality, apt to teach. One must notice that it takes time, and the experience of working under pressure, in order to confirm one's capacity to show moderation and self-restraint, to observe that one is rational and sensible in his actions and reactions, and to ascertain the level of one's neatness or methodical approach to handling the responsibilities of leadership. One's hospitality and one's ability to teach can only be demonstrated over time. Please note that just as there are leadership positions appropriate for single persons, there are also leadership positions appropriate for young people. Senior leaders, however, must be capable of making wise decisions in determining one's suitability for any leadership positions in which he or she is placed.

Paul continues to define what it takes to show that one is not a novice. In verse 5, he advises that such leader must have a previously established track record of (paraphrased) "not having been habitually engaged in loud arguments or physical altercations." Paul affirms that such leader must be old enough, and have been involved enough in life, to show that he is not harsh or rough in his actions and responses to others; but rather, he approaches things with a moderate temperament that lends itself to calmness, as opposed to causing or being likely to cause arguments, dissension, or controversy. Paul is clear that a good leader cannot be one whose reputation suggests that he is given to provoking arguments and contentions. Paul's final point in verse 3 (in paraphrase) is that "such leader must not be a person who loves money in a way that allows him to steal money, to cheat others out of their money, to be motivated by the prospect of money, to hoard money, to be stingy in his use of personal money, to promote schemes designed to extract money from his followers for his aggrandizement, or to manipulate circumstances for his own gain." A church leader must not be a lover of money!

Paul then points out that a person who cannot (in paraphrase) "manage his own home environment with efficiency and effectiveness," is indeed a novice. It is clear from the context of Paul's writing that the effective and efficient management of the home includes the subjection of offspring. Paul uses the term "gravity" in relationship to having the children "in subjection." While the matter of church leadership is no small feat, one can only be expected to handle it well if the pattern of the handling of his children is one that demonstrates seriousness and extreme importance, a manner that exhibits a sense of solemnity. My conclusion of this matter is the defining paradox raised in verse 5 (in paraphrase): "If a leader has not previously—prior to becoming a church leader—demonstrated the knowledge and the ability necessary in the management of his own house, and all that pertains to his house, why would we expect such person to have the necessary skill set and functional spirituality to lead the people of God in the church?"

A church leader must not be a novice!

Principle *33*

Church Leaders Must Lead by Example

...neither as being lords over God's heritage, but being ensamples to the flock. —1 Peter 5:3

Those things, which ye have both learned, and received, and heard, and seen in me, do: and the God of peace shall be with you. —Philippians 4:9

While not all persons appointed or elected to leadership positions within the church will have the advantage of being raised in the church since infancy, having that advantage can be of tremendous aid in one's appreciation of the role an example offers in the lives of others who may someday become leaders in the same church or the same network of churches. A godly example of how a person should behave in a given position is one of the best coaches for preparing those who may someday occupy that position. One of the most despicable occurrences in any church is when leaders behave in such a way that they fail to provide good examples for potential leaders. Having been raised in the church, I learned a great deal about the qualities of godly living from those whom I was privileged to watch while growing up. I learned what a good leader looks like; I learned how a good pastor acts before his congregation. In addition, because the pastor of my youth was also the bishop of the diocese, I was able to see firsthand what it looked like to be a good bishop. What a tremendous advantage! I did not have to look elsewhere to understand what leadership within the church, within the diocese, and within the organization should look like; I was able to see it all in real time.

Today, I find myself dismayed on two fronts. First, when leaders fail to realize the impact of their behavior on those watching from behind. Life has proven over and over that what is done in the dark will eventually come to the light. This is especially true in the life of the church, because Satan wishes to negatively expose the church every chance he gets. I have, unfortunately, had the displeasure of watching bad leaders as well. I am still haunted by the disturbing imagery of an experience from my youth involving a leader for whom I had great respect. I recall vividly, as if it were yesterday, that I was on a city bus going to visit a friend who lived eight or nine blocks away. As I disembarked from the bus at the corner of the street where my friend lived, I noticed several police cars. Being driven by the curiosity of my youth, I hung around to see what was going on. A few minutes later, I saw a great contingency of policemen come out of the store; I noticed a handcuffed man in the middle of them. As they got closer to me, I recognized the handcuffed man! To my utter amazement, I discovered that he was a minister, and one of the assistant pastors of the church my family attended; he served as the young people's president as well. I later learned that he had gone in and, at gunpoint, robbed the local confectionery on the corner.

I am also dismayed when senior leaders fail to hold secondary leaders accountable for behavior that brings reproach upon the church. The act of holding those leaders accountable sends a message to potential leaders that there is an expectation of excellence to which they must adhere. Such accountability also sends a message to followers, who must be taught to navigate the aftermath of such failures. We have almost developed a culture that excuses behavior that is inconsistent with the message of the church. Far too many church leaders have gotten away with reproachful acts of malfeasance, misfeasance, and nonfeasance. Some active church leaders have even gotten away with the type of behavior that the Bible speaks of by admonishing the church: *"Let it not be once named among you, as becometh saints..."* (Eph. 5:3).

The church is a unique assemblage of people. It has a dual responsibility of readily granting forgiveness for any failure to uphold the godly standards of behavior as handed down in Scripture, while holding those who fail to uphold such standards accountable. The moment the church ceases to forgive its offenders, it ceases to be a church. At the same time, the moment the church ceases to hold members to the Lord's standards, it ceases to be the Lord's church. Love, forgiveness, and restoration are as much a part of the gospel of Christ as sanctification and godly behavior. Paul cautioned the church: *"I beseech you therefore, brethren, by the mercies of God, that ye present your bodies a living sacrifice, holy, acceptable unto God, which is your reasonable service"* (Rom. 12:1).

Inherent in Paul's assertion was the note that this can only be done because of *"the mercies of God."* The church must teach such mercy as a main course at the altar of redemption and sanctification. As it does, the church must also teach sacrifice, holiness, and acceptability unto God. Just as the church cannot be passive in its expressions of mercy, it must also remain vigilant in its rebuke and reproof of negative behavior.

The church's inaction in the face of such behavior negates the biblical responsibility of leading by example. Peter fervently urged the leaders in the New Testament church to be examples to the flock. Failure to acknowledge and respect 1 Peter 5:3 is as irresponsible and disrespectful as one's failure to acknowledge and respect any other text that gives directions for those who desire to walk with God. When church leaders consistently engage in negative behavior, it not only cripples the church today, but it also does violence to tomorrow's church by its failure to provide strong positive examples for tomorrow's church leaders.

Church leaders must lead by example!

Principle 34

Church Leaders Must Bring Forth Fruit

...which is come unto you, as it is in all the world; and bringeth forth fruit, as it doth also in you, since the day ye heard of it, and knew the grace of God in truth ... that ye might walk worthy of the Lord unto all pleasing, being fruitful in every good work, and increasing in the knowledge of God.... —Colossians 1:6, 10

...being filled with the fruits of righteousness, which are by Jesus Christ, unto the glory and praise of God. —Philippians 1:11

For if these things be in you, and abound, they make you that ye shall neither be barren nor unfruitful in the knowledge of our Lord Jesus Christ. —2 Peter 1:8

I remember very vividly as a child in Sunday School listening to our teacher tell a story about Jesus and a fig tree. While listening more attentively than normal, I became filled with frustration over the details of the story. I remember asking myself over and over, "Why would Jesus do that?" At one point, I raised my hand to ask why, but, for some reason, the teacher never answered the question. I left that day more frustrated because I could not understand why Jesus did what He did. My problem was that we had a large fig tree at our house, and I liked it.

The story, as told by my teacher, went like this: "Jesus was coming back to His city one morning when He saw a fig tree on the side of the road. Realizing He was hungry, He went to get figs, but there were none; there were only leaves. Jesus got so angry at the tree that He said to it, *'You will never bear figs again.'* Suddenly the tree dried up."

For many years afterwards, whenever I thought of that story, I would think to myself, Jesus could have just told the tree to bear figs for Him. I could not get it out of my head; Jesus did not have to kill the tree forever. As I got older, somewhere between my junior and my senior high school years, I realized that the story was telling me that *I must do what God created me for.* The fig tree, created to bring forth figs, did not. So, it had no usefulness. Somehow, that simple story planted in me the urgency to make sure I did what God wanted me to do, and to the best of my ability. I suppose to some degree, that the experience at five years old was the beginning of many years of leadership in the church. Then, as now, God expects all of us to bring forth the fruit of His purpose in our lives.

Many years later, as I was preparing a sermon, I ran across what I thought was the same text that my teacher used during that character-shaping lesson for this often over-expressive five-year-old. While this newly discovered story did involve a fig tree that bore no figs, unlike the first one, its failure to fulfill its purpose went on for three years before finally the owner of the vineyard discovered its fruitlessness. This time, however, the order was to cut the tree down. Though approached differently, the principle was still clear: in the absence of fruit, its purpose was not being fulfilled. What value is a fig tree that produces no figs? What value is a church leader who will not lead the people of the church effectively? In both cases, the answer is a resounding, "None!"

The second fig tree story introduced an amazing revelation concerning one of the responsibilities of church leaders. When the vineyard owner, who represents the Lord of the church, gave the order to cut the tree down, he also gave a clarifying reason. He asked (from the perspective of the Common English Bible), *"Why should a non-productive fig tree continue depleting the soil's nutrients?"* The gardener, a prototype of church leaders of any church, any church related organization, or any leader in a regional, national, or international church position, responded, *"Lord, give it one more year, and I will dig around it and give it fertilizer. Maybe it will produce fruit next year."*

A church leader's job is, among other things, to do what is necessary to successfully bring those who follow his or her leadership into a productive relationship with Jesus Christ! I am familiar with churches, or church-based organizations, where the job descriptions and all the sordid details of the functions of leadership were clearly written out. However, I have never seen a church leader's job description that listed the responsibilities of "digging around and fertilizing non-productive members or sub-leaders." But Jesus's emphasis on fig trees in the synoptic Gospels, and in some epistles, suggests that bringing forth fruit is of great importance in the work of church leadership. The church leader in the pericope of Luke's gospel understood that he must produce fruit at any cost.

> *A man owned a fig tree planted in his vineyard. He came looking for fruit on it and found none. He said to his gardener, "Look, I've come looking for fruit on this fig tree for the past three years, and I've never found any. Cut it down! Why should it continue depleting the soil's nutrients?" The gardener responded, "Lord, give it one*

> *more year, and I will dig around it and give it fertilizer.*
> *Maybe it will produce fruit next year; if not, then you*
> *can cut it down."* (Luke 13:6–9 CEB)

What good is an auxiliary leader who cannot lead an auxiliary? What good is a department head who has difficulty heading a department? What good is there in an administrator who simply does not, or cannot, administer? What good is a pastor who cannot effectively pastor the church? What good is a diocese or regional officer who simply cannot do the job? What good is a bishop who cannot successfully lead the diocese? I thank God that He has placed within the vineyard of His church leaders at every level whose responsibility is to assist in all areas of development. Perhaps those words, *"Lord, give it one more year,"* are suggestive that the order to *"cut the tree down"* has been put off until the tree is dug around and fertilized with the nutrients of the Holy Spirit.

Church leaders must bring forth fruit!

Principle 35

Church Leaders Must Walk Worthy of Their Call

I therefore, the prisoner of the Lord, beseech you that ye walk worthy of the vocation wherewith ye are called.
—Ephesians 4:1

...that ye would walk worthy of God, who hath called you unto his kingdom and glory. —1 Thessalonians 2:12

Apostle Paul called upon both the church at Ephesus and the church at Thessalonica to live worthy of a status that looms larger than the life of those to whom he wrote. The instructions are as applicable today as they were the day they were written. The validity of Paul's instructions must never be questioned by those who would dare to align themselves with the cause of Christ; this is especially important for those who wear the garments of church leadership. Paul's admonition for saints of the Ephesian church was that they walk worthy of the vocation wherewith they were called.

It is interesting that Paul used the word "vocation" when addressing a group of people whose work was often performed without the benefit of monetary compensation. It would seem that the word "avocation" would be more appropriate as a designation for work for which the laborer is not being paid a salary or stipend. Just what is the difference between one's vocation and one's avocation? The most commonly accepted definition of the word "vocation" since 1908 is that it speaks to a person's employment or main occupation, one's trade or profession. Conversely, the most commonly accepted definition of the word "avocation" speaks to a person's hobby or something that one enjoys without regard to compensation; it speaks to a secondary or less important line of engagement.

America's attitude towards working for pay versus working as an act of charity shifted as a result of the work of a Boston, Massachusetts, civil engineer and attorney by the name of Frank Parsons, who is credited with the establishment of Vocational Guidance. Within a few years, the movement officially evolved into what became the National Vocational Guidance Association. As a result of the association's firm commitment to the idea of the relationship of work with earnings, the use of the term "vocation" also evolved. This caused a universal evolution of the semantic reference to the term's religious meanings in everyday usage.

While Paul's reference to "vocation" in Ephesians 4 was more in line with the original inferences of the word as used in early church settings, one must consider the factual reality that words are defined by contemporary nuances as opposed to original semantics. At the risk of sounding like an etymologist, one who studies the origin and evolution of words, it would be helpful to look at the comparison between the two words, "vocation" versus "avocation," from the context of the earlier languages from which they surfaced. The word "vocation" evolved from *vocare*, which means "to call"; whereas the word "avocation" evolved from *avocare*, which means "call away"! The former word speaks to a divine calling, such as to be called by God into a specific work. Areas of such calling could be the church, the humanities, charitable endeavors, or anything that benefits mankind or brings aid to the sufferings of mankind. Paul's original statement of Ephesians 4:1 would be rendered: *"I therefore, the prisoner of the Lord, beseech you that ye walk worthy of the [calling] wherewith ye are called."*

The next question raised by this text, along with the Thessalonians text, is regarding the implications of "worthy." What does it mean to walk worthy of one's calling? What does it mean to walk worthy of God? First, let's examine a practical definition of what it means to be worthy. To walk worthy, which are the instructions of both texts, means that one is to "demonstrate the qualities that are expected by one's position!" Of course, I am sure we can all agree on the prerequisite requirement that to demonstrate a behavior, one must have the ability of such behavior; subsequently, one must show such ability. In like manner, one must possess the innate qualities, the characteristics, and the character required of such behavior.

Simply stated concerning the Ephesian text, what does the church in which you serve expect of their leaders? And more specifically, what does the church expect of *your* leadership? In more than fifty years of leadership in the church, and having visited, as guest preacher or teacher, more than five hundred churches or church conferences throughout the world, I have discovered that every church has its own unique character and idiosyncratic culture. This goes beyond the local church; it is also true for organizations, and separate entities that service the church community.

While there are some distinct advantages in selecting leaders from within the church entity that he is going to serve, there are occasions when it is necessary to bring a prospective leader from a different church community to serve another such entity. One of the main advantages of an inside leader is that he is already familiar with the character of such church and is already a part of its culture.

For those who are imported into an established church or church organization, I strongly recommend that you take time to learn the culture and character of the church into which you are called to serve. One of the biggest mistakes made by newly appointed leaders is that in their haste to amalgamate themselves into the organization, they often ignore its existing culture. That could result in chaos that is reminiscent of a "brand war" in a business organization where every newly appointed leader seeks to implement his brand of leadership. In a business organization, where the objective is monetary profit, as opposed to the development and enrichment of spirituality, this might be acceptable; but such behavior can never become the intrinsic modus operandi of the church. While money is certainly necessary to fund the operations of the church, money must never become its primary objective!

In church leadership, it is imperative that new leaders move thoughtfully as they seek to implement change. This rule of thumb applies to both necessary change—change that directly enhances an "impaired" viability of the institution—which is often the reason a new leader was appointed, and what I call "cosmetic operational change." Cosmetic operational change refers to change that does not directly enhance the organization's ability to successfully perform its duties; rather, it is change that does more for the leader's image and reputation than for the church. In making change in the way an existing church operates, we must be careful not to typecast the church as if its practices and procedures were ineffective or out of step with some "new reality" prior to the new leader's arrival. It would be good if every church leader would remember that the church was in existence long before you came along and will probably be in existence long after you are gone.

This does not suggest that change is innately negative; this is intended merely to emphasize caution during that "sacred period" between the new leader's arrival and his acceptance by the group he is to lead. Once the "honeymoon" is over, the leader is, in the jargon of the airline industry, free to move about the cabin. I still recommend caution when moving about in the area of change! Most churches and church institutions are riddled with "sacred cows" that stir up dust when moved in the slightest way. I have consulted with, and represented, leaders whose tenure was threatened because a much needed "turn" was a bit too sharp.

The question raised of the Thessalonians text is: What does *God* expect of those whom He calls into the leadership of His church? Anyone who has enjoyed a longtime relationship with Scripture could recite several characteristics, attitudes, mindsets, dispositions, abstinences, and overall good behavior that God, in His infallible Word, requires of both leaders and followers alike. The Old Testament prophet Micah said it best: *"He hath shewed thee, O man, what is good; and what doth the Lord require of thee, but to do justly, and to love mercy, and to walk humbly with thy God?"* (Mic. 6:8).

The answer to Paul's instructions to the Thessalonian church that they walk worthy of God can be summed up in three all-inclusive areas as stated in Micah 6:8. When followed, such adherence will render one worthy of God's imputation of worthiness. It must be understood by all who lead the people of God that their worthiness can never be self-actualized; rather, such status is always an act of God's grace. For only God can deem us worthy. To the church at Philippi, Paul writes, *"For it is God which worketh in you both to will and to do of his good pleasure"* (Phil. 2:13). God, by virtue of His worthiness, ascribes worthiness onto church leaders whom He has chosen. Such imputation is His recompense to their commitment to do justly and to love mercy, and to walk humbly with God.

Church leaders must walk worthy of their call!

It must be understood by all who lead the people of God that their worthiness can never be self-actualized; rather, such status is always an act of God's grace.

Principle 36

Church Leaders Must Be Blameless

...according as he hath chosen us in him before the foundation of the world, that we should be holy and without blame before him in love. —Ephesians 1:4

And you, that were sometime alienated and enemies in your mind by wicked works, yet now hath he reconciled in the body of his flesh through death, to present you holy and unblameable and unreproveable in his sight.
—Colossians 1:22

Abstain from all appearance of evil. And the very God of peace sanctify you wholly; and I pray God your whole spirit and soul and body be preserved blameless unto the coming of our Lord Jesus Christ.
—1 Thessalonians 5:22–23

A bishop then must be blameless, the husband of one wife, vigilant, sober, of good behaviour, given to hospitality, apt to teach.... And let these also first be proved; then let them use the office of a deacon, being found blameless.
—1 Timothy 3:2, 10

If any be blameless, the husband of one wife, having faithful children not accused of riot or unruly. For a bishop must be blameless, as the steward of God; not selfwilled, not soon angry, not given to wine, no striker, not given to filthy lucre....   —Titus 1:6–7

The responsibility of church leaders to maintain a state of blamelessness in the conduct of life was well noted in the early church. This requirement is mentioned in some Pauline epistles in reference to leaders such as bishops and deacons. However, it is important to note the New Testament's use of the word "bishop" is slightly different from that of today's church. In the New Testament church, the person who served as the overseer, or leading clergy, who was responsible for its day-to-day operational activities, was referred to by the title of bishop. However, in many denominations today, the title of bishop is reserved for clergy designated by his denominational authorities as the head of a diocese or jurisdiction.

In some cases, such as Ephesians 4, general members of the New Testament church were encouraged that they *"should be holy and without blame before him in love."* Having addressed this concept of blamelessness during conferences and/or conventions in various parts of the country, I have often been questioned about the validity of being able to escape the frivolous accusations that are sometimes levied against those who hold positions of leadership. Of course, such questions are raised about leaders both within and outside of the church. "How can," I'm often asked, "someone be held responsible for charges of things they are accused of without any proof that such things were actually done by the accused person?"

That is a valid question! It is particularly valid considering the "Me too" movement that has exploded across America, and the world, during recent years. As has been argued by many accused persons, such accusations were often about events and actions that were alleged to have taken place decades before. While the passing of time does not negate the responsibility of illegal acts, if such acts were committed by the accused in the manner charged, the passage of time often obscures the memory of both the victim and the accused perpetrator. And, even worse, in some cases, it's difficult to find credible witnesses whose recollection of events and circumstances have not been clouded by the passage of time.

In most biblical references to blamelessness, the question is not centered on the accusations; rather, the question is centered on the credibility of the conduct of the person accused. The primary question is: Does the accused conduct himself in a way that supports such accusation? The biblical idea of blamelessness is concerned with patterns of conduct and prior practices engaged in by the leader. Does his lifestyle give credence to such accusation? That is the question that either constitutes or invalidates the idea of blame or blamelessness.

One can infer from the Colossians text above, that the status of being *"holy and unblameable and unreproveable in his [God's] sight"* comes because of being *"reconciled in the body of his flesh through death."* This is evident because the reconciled person at the end of the verse is the same person who, at the beginning of the verse, is described as, *"And you, that were sometime alienated and enemies in your mind by wicked works."*

The church generally accepts the idea that judgment begins at the house of the Lord; as such, acts of wrongdoing prior to our relationship with Christ are exonerated. We are thus absolved from blame for such wrongdoing. Our status of blamelessness comes because of God's saving grace.

Paul beseeched the Thessalonians to *"hold fast that which is good. Abstain from all appearance of evil. And the very God of peace sanctify you wholly...."* As he closed the verse, Paul prayed that their *"whole spirit and soul and body be preserved blameless unto the coming of our Lord Jesus Christ."*

In both 1 Timothy and Titus, Paul's reference to one's blamelessness is accompanied by a litany of behavioral responsibilities that were to be integrated into the lifestyle of the bishop and the deacon. Such behavior would place the compliant leader in the position of not lending himself to the legitimacy of any charges that might be brought against him. By his actions or lifestyle, such leader then insulates himself against the possibility that any reasonable accusation could be sustained.

Church leaders must be blameless!

Principle 37

Church Leaders Must Be Faithful

Moreover it is required in stewards, that a man be found faithful. —1 Corinthians 4:2

And the Lord said, Who then is that faithful and wise steward, whom his Lord shall make ruler over his household, to give them their portion of meat in due season?
—Luke 12:42

There are three renderings in this book on principles involving some aspect of faith. In addition to this principle, whereby "Church Leaders Must Be Faithful," other such principles are: "Church Leaders Must Demonstrate a Measure of Faith"; and "Church Leaders Must Be Grounded in the Faith"! All three renderings approach the faith challenges from slightly different nuances. One is to be faithful; another is to show faith; the final one is to be grounded in faith. Each aspect of faith is quite essential to church leadership. It would be foolish of me, or any author, to attempt to categorize them by order of importance. They are all important, and without any one of them, it would be difficult to please God, and impossible to excel in the ministry of church leadership.

Let's look at what it means for a church leader to be faithful. The Latin word from which the word "faith" was derived was originally understood to be without any direct association to deity or religious beliefs. In the Greco-Roman culture, faith was used to denote confidence or trust in a person, thing, or idea. Faith was an expression of trust, belief, confidence, conviction, credence, reliance, and expectation from one person concerning another person, thing, or idea. As such, to *"be found faithful,"* as the phrase is projected by Apostle Paul in 1 Corinthians 4:2, speaks to the conclusion drawn by others regarding such person. The implication of the phrase now speaks to the quality of performance of one's responsibility, and the continued fulfillment of such responsibility. When the work of such steward is reviewed, he must be found to have satisfactorily performed and maintained a credible level of responsibility.

While Paul gives no definitive indication as to who the "reviewer" is, one can subsume that the ultimate reviewer is God Himself. In more user-friendly versions of this text, Paul seems to be rebutting the idea that others can judge his work. He concludes with the statement that God will judge, and that is the only judgment about which he is concerned. The Common English Bible presents the text as follows:

> *So a person should think about us this way—as servants of Christ and managers of God's secrets. In this kind of situation, what is expected of a manager is that they prove to be faithful. I couldn't care less if I'm judged by you or by any human court; I don't even judge myself. I'm not aware of anything against me, but that doesn't make me innocent, because the Lord is the one who judges me. So don't judge anything before the right time—wait until the Lord comes. He will bring things that are hidden in the dark to light, and he will make people's motivations public. Then there will be recognition for each person from God.* (1 Corinthians 4:1–5 CEB)

Church leaders are stewards of the highest order. As such, being faithful is not an optional decision. Paul uses, in the King James Version of the text, the phrase, *"it is required of a steward... "*! The term "required" leaves no room for any discretionary interpretation; "required" denotes the lack of any other alternative. Required behavior is considered compulsory; it is indispensable. Does this mean that the steward who is not found faithful will simply be relieved of his duties as a steward? To the contrary, in the parable of the talents, wherein the lord of the vineyard gave his talents to his servants. The pericope reveals that each servant, except for the servant who received one talent, made full use of his stewardship to the extent that two servants doubled that for which they were responsible.

On the day of reckoning, when the lord encountered the unfaithful servant who buried his lord's talent and stated out of fear: *"I knew thee that thou art an hard man, reaping where thou hast not sown, and gathering where thou hast not strawed: and I was afraid, and went and hid thy talent in the earth: lo, there thou hast that is thine"* (Matt. 25:24–25).

Here, the narrative takes a turn for the worse:

> *His Lord answered and said unto him, Thou wicked and slothful servant, thou knewest that I reap where I sowed not, and gather where I have not strawed: thou oughtest therefore to have put my money to the exchangers, and then at my coming I should have received mine own with usury. Take therefore the talent from him, and give it unto him which hath ten talents ... And cast ye the unprofitable servant into outer darkness: there shall be weeping and gnashing of teeth.* (Matthew 25:26–28, 30)

We cannot attest the extent to which this symbolic representation will be carried out at the day of reckoning; however, the text does convey that the judgment will be unpleasant for those who are judged thereby. The reality is that punitive judgment can be easily avoided by simply performing our stewardship duties within the expected standards, by being faithful. The choice of the assignment is the prerogative of God; however, the choice of the level of performance is wholly that of the steward—the church leader.

My advice to those already functional in the leadership of the church, as well as to those who longingly desire for such placement, is to evaluate both your spiritual and your psychological ability to make the necessary commitments to the requirements of the task before going any further. Once placed into the Lord's service, it is irreversible. In the event one has already encountered failure in the quality of his performance as a leader, such failure is forgivable; the necessary commitments can be made; sufficient grace can be applied; the steward can be found faithful from such point forward.

Church leaders must be faithful to the tasks to which they are assigned. This is inclusive of all components that are part and parcel of the assignment. Generally speaking, such components are not nearly as exciting as the assignment itself, but they are often prerequisite to the assignment. No matter how exciting the primary assignment appears, these prerequisites are required as prior conditions before any other activity can take place. There may be a tendency to dislike the minutia of the project among personality types who are commonly classified as those who become good leaders; however, the details that are a part of the ultimate project are as important as the project itself. Often, they become the foundation upon which the project is built. Church leaders must be faithful to the performance of both the nonessentials and the main assignment.

Another boring element that church leaders must guard against is the repetitive nature of tasks that must be performed routinely. While something may be exciting the first half dozen times it is performed, somewhere around the twentieth time it becomes rather mundane. After a while, there often develops a tendency to treat such things as if they are bothersome; in some cases, however, one does not realize the stabilizing aspect of such repetitive functions to those who make up the group. Psychologists may argue that such regular occurrences tend to soothe the anxieties and apprehensions of people who suffer from some types of neurosis. Such people may find security in such repetitiveness. This does not suggest that innovative ideas and practices cannot be introduced to the group; however, one must not discard essential activities based upon his reluctance to enjoy such activities.

Church leaders must be faithful!

Church leaders must be faithful to the performance of both the nonessentials and the main assignment.

Principle *38*

Church Leaders Must Be Pleasing to God

Wherewith shall I come before the Lord, and bow my-self before the high God? shall I come before him with burnt offerings, with calves of a year old? Will the Lord be pleased with thousands of rams, or with ten thousands of rivers of oil? shall I give my firstborn for my transgression, the fruit of my body for the sin of my soul?
—Micah 6:6–7

In the above text, the prophet Micah expresses his willingness to do anything to please God. He raises the question, "Will the Lord be pleased…?" Of course, his plea was under the plan of salvation of a dispensation that differs greatly from the "dispensation of grace" as revealed in the New Testament plan of salvation. Whereas, the new covenant ushered in a "grace-based" plan of salvation, one executed by faith as opposed to the multiple offerings that our Old Testament brothers and sisters were required to present before the Lord. The thing that has not changed is the absolute necessity of bringing one's life into conformity with the wishes of God. In other words, despite the change in the administration of God's salvific relationship with humanity, man must always strive to please God.

The more we understand the mechanics of salvation, the more inclined we will become to committing to a lifestyle of pleasing God. While the flames of such commitment may start out ever so bright, they may be quenched from time to time by the blustering winds of discouragement. It is incumbent upon mid-level church leaders to keep the flames of their fire burning at full capacity so that the manifestation of God's response to the leader's flame will serve as an encouragement to the laity. As leaders climb the ladder of church leadership, the urgency of a noticeably visible commitment to the fires of others is more crucial. Romans 15:1 confirms that responsibility: *"We then that are strong ought to bear the infirmities of the weak, and not to please ourselves"* (Rom. 15:1).

In Apostle Paul's epistle to the church at Thessalonica, he speaks of the relationship between one's godly walk and pleasing God, *"so ye would abound more and more."* Paul seems to suggest that God responds to those who please Him. In fact, inherent in the nuance of the word "abound" is the indication of overflow or abundance. In the context of leadership, such a word would denote moving up in rank, status, and relationship. The use of the term "more and more" simply adds clarity to the abundance of the leader's anticipated overflow which results from his commitment to, above all else, please God.

As far back as the early times of the Old Testament, the Bible says of Enoch, *"For before his translation he had this testimony, that he pleased God"* (Heb. 11:5). The writer of the Hebrews reminded the Hebrew saints of Enoch's abundance and overflow, his moving up in rank. While I have never witnessed one's physical translation from earth into the heavenly presence of God during my sixty years of leadership experience, I have seen the abundant presence of God in the lives of those leaders whose commitment to His pleasure guided their actions.

Principle 38: Must Be Pleasing to God

One of the key factors in the experience of such "God pleasure" is the evident management of one's flesh. The ability to bring the flesh into subjection to the spirit is a blessing in and of itself. Paul wrote extensively about the struggle between the flesh and the spirit; he understood the need to overcome the compulsions of the flesh in favor of that which edifies the spirit. Paul's objective was to live pleasingly before God; he understood that he could not please God as long as he operated according to the flesh. He shared with the saints at Rome, *"So then they that are in the flesh cannot please God. But ye are not in the flesh, but in the Spirit, if so be that the Spirit of God dwell in you. Now if any man have not the Spirit of Christ, he is none of his"* (Rom. 8:8–9).

Just as Paul wrestled with his flesh, many conscientious church leaders experience similar conflicts as they go about the task of caring for, and leading, the people of God. One reason for such conflict is that Satan attempts to derail the work of God by debilitating the church of God. Satan is acutely aware that if those who struggle are going to be strengthened, it will be because of the fellowship, the intercession, and the testimonies of the saints. The forces of evil seek to disable that which does the most good.

Because the church is designed for the care of the saints, its success comes from the good working order of all its systems. The various levels of leadership God has placed in the church is reminiscent of an indigenous care center. It is a hospital of sorts where the leaders and members are each other's keepers; where the brothers and sisters are all accountable for each other; where, if one is overtaken in a fault, the others seek to restore him in a spirit of love and meekness. God designed the church to be a New Testament "City of Refuge" for those who find themselves victims of the cruelty of satanic revenge.

Church leaders, at all levels, must comprehend the vastness of the task of which they are a very integral part. Church leaders must not be dismissive of their great responsibility in the maintenance and upkeep of those who depend upon such leadership for the survival of their soul. The Lord's church is the Lord's method of preserving those whose trust is in Him. Please be advised that any leader who, whether voluntarily or involuntarily, neglects his responsibility in this great network of care, displeases God. Such failure to please God results in the leader forfeiting the blessings of God upon his or her life.

Church leaders must be pleasing to God!

Principle 39

Church Leaders Must Learn to Be Content

For I have learned, in whatsoever state I am, therewith to be content. I know both how to be abased, and I know how to abound: every where and in all things I am instructed both to be full and to be hungry, both to abound and to suffer need. —Philippians 4:11–12

One of mankind's most self-destructive attitudes is the insatiable desire for more. It often seems as if the more one gets, the more one wants. There is nothing inherently wrong about wanting to advance in life. However, the desire to get a newer one, a bigger one, or just another one can push some people into the dark corners of "super greed" and ravenous behavior—avarice. Avarice is a dysfunction that infects upon its subject an extreme greed for wealth and material possessions. Such extreme greed is not in fulfillment of need; rather, simply for the sake of having more. The sad irony is that the primary purpose for wanting more is often to stand out among one's peers. While avarice is not of itself a mental disorder, it is a grave symptom of an underlying psychological issue. There is no place for such behavior among church leaders!

According to the *Encyclopedia of World Problems and Human Potential*:

Avarice is a state in which an individual attaches such value to wealth and possessions that he makes the accumulation and retention of them the major goal of life, to which he subordinates all else. It is not a normal human instinct; it is imposed by a materialistic society. It substitutes possessing for living. In a state of avarice, the individual's life is so devoid of internal meaning that he creates personal significance with external things. It leads to a distorted view of reality and a harmful narrowing of vision and imagination. Because it has no limit to its desire to do and to have, it disregards the property and rights of others. It involves a sense of ambition and purpose without limit. Such perversion of values is totally disruptive of the moral life.[6]

While the problem of greed, selfishness, aggressive hostility, cheating, and general savageness—all of which are inherent in an attitude of super greed—is not new, its intensity has grown to such proportion that it presents a plethora of new problems for society. We see its ugly results in every aspect of human existence, from selfish toddlers inconsiderately holding on to multiple toys while other crying toddlers are hindered from having access to any of them, to adult shoppers fighting to purchase large amounts of sale items while others wait to claim one or two. It is not unusual to see signs in big box stores limiting the number of a single item one can purchase.

Whereas, during years past, larger churches were built because congregational growth demanded more space; in recent years, larger churches were built simply to have a larger church. The result is that we are seeing large churches that are only half filled. The need for more has become its own end. The problem is that there is no

---

6   Mankind 2000, (1986). *Encyclopedia of World Problems and Human Potential.* The Union of International Associations

logic by which one can measure rhyme or reason. From churches that are far bigger than necessity demands, to bigger homes with fewer occupants, bigger and more cars, multiple fur coats, more shoes and clothes than the closets in an average home can hold, a different watch for every day of the week, to more, more, more, and even more.

Where does this insatiable desire for more end? And when is bigger, big enough? Apostle Paul partially described this phenomenon as *"perverse disputings of men of corrupt minds, and destitute of the truth, supposing that gain is godliness..."* (1 Tim. 6:5). Paul's advice concerning such compromised reasoning is, *"From such withdraw thyself."*

Avarice is not the only answer; there is an alternative theology! Paul continues by saying, *"But godliness with contentment is great gain."* He reasons, *"For we brought nothing into this world, and it is certain we can carry nothing out. And having food and raiment, let us be therewith content."* Paul concludes this narrative of 1 Timothy 6:5–11, by raising three final points. They are:

1. *But they that will be rich fall into temptation and a snare, and into many foolish and hurtful lusts, which drown men in destruction and perdition.*

2. *For the love of money is the root of all evil: which while some coveted after, they have erred from the faith, and pierced themselves through with many sorrows.*

3. *But thou, O man of God, flee these things; and follow after righteousness, godliness, faith, love, patience, meekness.*

Notice Paul's reference to Timothy in the third point. *"But thou, O man of God..."* Without question, Timothy was a church leader! Could it be that Paul's advice is not given to Timothy alone, but collectively to all who serve in the leadership of the church? The need for purity of service from church leaders demands freedom from being ensnared in greed and excessiveness. The quest for more of the same must give way to the spirituality of contentment. He shared with the leaders and members of the Philippian church, *"For I have learned, in whatsoever state I am, therewith to be content. I know both how to be abased, and I know how to abound: every where and in all things I am instructed both to be full and to be hungry, both to abound and to suffer need"* (Phil. 4:11–12).

While Paul's lesson of contentment was not an easy one; indeed, it was learned from the school of humility. It was learned from the school of rejection. Paul's contentment was learned from the school of suffering at the hands of followers who rebelled against his leadership. It was learned from the school of punitive authorities whose lifestyle Paul's preaching condemned. However learned, the lesson of contentment is mandatory for those who will graduate into the leadership of the Lord's church.

Church leaders must learn to be content!

Principle 40

Church Leaders Must Be Willing to Forget the Past

Brethren, I count not myself to have apprehended: but this one thing I do, forgetting those things which are behind, and reaching forth unto those things which are before, I press toward the mark for the prize of the high calling of God in Christ Jesus. —Philippians 13–14

There is a text in the Bible where Jesus evaluates the value of a person who *"puts his hand on the plough, and looking back..."* While looking back can have precautionary characteristics, particularly as it relates to safety, the generally accepted nuance of looking back speaks to a sense of regret, a feeling of missing out on something, or missing something. The person whose intentions appear to be locked on yesterday will have a difficult time navigating the responsibilities of today.

> *And Jesus said unto him, No man, having put his hand to the plough, and looking back, is fit for the kingdom of God.* (Luke 9:62)

Luke's narrative comes at the end of a long litany of problems and probable solutions. He quotes the wisdom of Jesus throughout the chapter as the essence of several real-time solutions. The chapter begins with Jesus calling the disciples together to give them power over devils, the authority to cure diseases, and to send them out to preach and heal. In other words, Jesus sent His disciples out to function in the capacity of church leaders! Here are twelve newly chosen and commissioned leaders about to embark upon the most important assignments of their lives. An observant person may notice the stipulations placed upon the disciples by the commissioning agent—Jesus Christ:

> *Then he called his twelve disciples together, and gave them power and authority over all devils, and to cure diseases. And he sent them to preach the kingdom of God, and to heal the sick.* (Luke 9:1–2)

First, Jesus gave them power *over* all devils; He did not give them power to *control* those devils. Instead, He gave them power to *supersede* or *reverse* what the devils did. This coincides with a corresponding assertion by Apostle John: *"Ye are of God, little children, and have overcome them: because greater is he that is in you, than he that is in the world"* (1 John 4:4). It is important to note that even in today's church, with all its electronic gadgetry, leaders cannot control the demonic activities of the devils who seek to disrupt the work of the church. Contrary to what many leaders would have members believe, you can rebuke such devils; you can resist them, but you absolutely cannot control them! The solution put in place by Jesus for such lack of control is that leaders are given power and authority over the devils. I strongly encourage church leaders to take full advantage of such authority in dealing with the devils who, for the most part, are like pesky flies; the greatest damage they do is the irritation they cause.

The next stipulation placed upon them was in their power and authority to cure diseases. Two things are worthy of mention; first, they were to *cure* the disease, not bandage it, impede it, or gloss over it, but to cure it. To "cure" means the person is relieved of the symptoms of the disease; it means the elimination of the disease, to restore such person back to good health. The second thing worth mentioning here is what qualifies as a disease. A disease is a structural disorder that has a known cause and a distinctive group of signs, symptoms, or anatomical changes. A disease can also be classified as a function, habit, or disposition that causes an adverse effect upon a person.

I suggest that from a syntactical order, in the placement of the wording of the curing of diseases, the placement of the word "devils" follows. This might suggest that diseases follow the devil, or the devil causes diseases. If so, then, we could surmise that if we get rid of the devils in one's life, we inevitably get rid of the diseases in one's life.

Another stipulation placed upon the disciples—a prototype of today's church leaders—is that of *what* they were empowered to preach. Jesus did not give them the authority to preach anything they *wanted* to preach, or things that they felt good about preaching. They were not at liberty to preach those things that made them popular; neither could they focus on those things that the people desired to hear. They could not decide that, since people want to be healthy and wealthy, then they would preach health and wealth. As important as praise and worship is, that, as a freestanding activity, was not part of the commission given here by Jesus to those leaders. They were given a very narrow parameter within which they were to preach. Of course, my use of the word "narrow" speaks only to subject matter, because the kingdom of God is broad enough to cover every aspect of human existence, then, now, and eternally.

The point here is that church leaders are required to preach the kingdom of God. As a former adjunct professor of preaching, I advised students that if their preaching did not "reside within" the kingdom of God, it did not fall within the category of gospel preaching. By residing within the kingdom of God, I am suggesting that preaching must be directly or passively connected with the kingdom of God. One of the primary purposes of preaching is to bring sinners to Christ. This is important because both disease and sickness reside in the domain of sin. Again, if we eradicate sin, we conversely eradicate sickness and disease.

Following Jesus's "what to preach" instructions, He then authorized His disciples to heal the sick. Like the word "cure," the word "heal" speaks to causing a person to become sound and healthy again. This involves both physical and mental sickness, and thus, physical and mental healing. I suggest that when the kingdom of God is wholly and effectively preached by those authorized of God to do so, both the physical and mental health of those who receive such preaching will be drastically improved. I teach that when preaching is properly executed, it not only challenges the lifestyles of those who listen, but it becomes a means of therapeutic help to those who struggle in the realm of mental anxiety. Of course, this does not displace those whom God has made available to His people for such help; however, it does provide a layer of protection against the actions of devils in their efforts to nullify the well-being of God's people. Please take notice that where the disciples preached, healing accompanied them: *"And they departed, and went through the towns, preaching the gospel, and healing every where"* (Luke 9:6).

As the narrative of Luke 9 unfolds, Jesus illustrates that the pursuit of the kingdom of God can, and should, be elevated to a position where it is the most important endeavor of all mankind. And, for those called into its service, as leaders of the church, it is imperative that they hold the activities of the church in highest regard. Here, Jesus used hyperbolic analogies to confirm His expectation of such regard in the hearts and minds of those whom he called into leadership. In one case, He stressed that the work of the kingdom of God is more important than the assumed necessities of life. In another case, Jesus illustrated that the relationship of the kingdom of God to the affairs of life is beyond all other human relationships. In His final analysis, Jesus used the hyperbole of the servant who plows while looking back.

The idea of looking back is symptomatic of several compromising positions for those engaged in the leadership of the church. Inclusive of such compromise is how we look at our achievements in relation to the achievements of others. Leaders must be careful of comparing what they have attained in life, no matter how necessary such things are perceived to be, with what their peers have attained. God does not bless us because of the category to which we belong; God blesses us because of our contributions to the work of His kingdom, and our commitment thereto. Those who value their achievements or accomplishments as being equal to, or greater than, the value of their functions within the kingdom of God, are unfit for the kingdom of God.

Another compromising mindset that impedes the progress of church leaders is how they respond to the implications of their responsibilities to relatives and friends. As a church leader of several decades, I have seen leaders abdicate their responsibilities because of demands placed upon them by close friends or relatives. I have even seen church leaders steal church money because a family member had a financial emergency. I have known cases where a church leader made equipment, dedicated to church use, available to relatives or friends for use in the most ungodly settings. A model of such blasphemous behavior is shown in the Old Testament, along with the punishment God meted out. Church leaders must measure the possible impact of the activities requested of family members and friends (and church members as well) against their responsibility to the image required of their leadership position.

The final compromising mindset church leaders must guard against lies in the subtle inferences that suggest some sense of feeling as if he is missing something by committing to the rigors of church leadership. One must not allow his attitude to suggest that by assuming a leadership position, he or she will not be able to enjoy the fun previously had when living under less stringent requirements. Church leaders must be careful not to give off an aura of regret as they move about the church. Such disposition displays an undeniable atmosphere that seems to negatively influence those who interact with such leaders.

As stated by Apostle Paul in his letter to the Philippian church, before anyone, church leader or otherwise, can reach forth unto those things which are before, and press towards the mark for the prize of the high calling of God in Christ Jesus, he or she must learn to forget those things that are behind. Such persons must erase all vestiges that give off indications of longing for their past, or that suggest they miss, with regret, the activities of a previous lifestyle. For such person, said Jesus, is not *"fit for the kingdom of God."*

In the process of eradicating any suggestions of longing for past experiences, church leaders must also be willing to give up the hurts of the past. Those things that caused bad feelings to take permanent residence in the memory of such leaders; those memories that continue to generate animosity against former offenders, even though such offenses may be real—still, the resulting anger must be eradicated. The burden of the baggage of past hurt will create far more weight on the leader than on the person who caused the hurt. The church leader who cannot let such things go is equally unfit for the kingdom of God!

> *Brethren, I count not myself to have apprehended: but this one thing I do, forgetting those things which are behind, and reaching forth unto those things which are*

Principle 40: Must Be Willing to Forget the Past

before, I press toward the mark for the prize of the high calling of God in Christ Jesus. (Philippians 3:13–14)

Church leaders must be willing to forget the past!

If You Are Enjoying This Book, Will You Help Me Spread the Word?

There are several ways you can help me get the word out about the message of this book…

- Visit my website, and leave a review: 52principlesforchurchleaders.com

- Recommend the book to friends and fellow church leaders. Word of mouth is still the more effective form of advertising.

- Purchase additional copies to give away as gifts.

- Post a 5-Star review on Amazon, Goodreads and other places that come to mind.

- Write about the book on your Facebook, Twitter, Instagram, Google+, any social media sites you regularly use.

- Post a photo of yourself with the book on your social media.

- Ask bookstores if they carry the book. If not, they can easily order it through all major distributors.

- If you blog, consider referencing the book, or publishing an excerpt from the book with a link back to the website where you bought it.

- Do you know a podcaster, journalist or media personality who might be willing to interview me or write an article based on the book?

- Contact me by email at 52principlesbook@gmail.com.

Principle *41*

Church Leaders Must Follow Protocol

But all things must be done appropriately and in an orderly manner. —1 Corinthians 14:40 (AMP)

In church, as in life, there are usually multiple ways to accomplish the tasks that circumstances require. To state it casually, there is a right way, there is a wrong way, there is an easy way, there is a hard way, there is everyone else's way, there is the usual way, there is the generally accepted way, and there is the way your church wants it done. The way your church wants it done is called "the protocol"! Protocol can be defined as the way an organization has established for the performance of its routine activities. Because a protocol has been established, does not mean there are no other ways by which the same task can be performed. Quite the contrary, it simply means that this is the way "we" want it done.

In some institutions, much of its protocol has been codified into written rules that are easy to ascertain, understand, and follow. On the other hand, there are protocols that have been established by precedent that may not exist in writing, but everyone is expected to follow those time-honored traditions. This is when protocol can become confusing, and at times, problematic. There are three very essential rules pertaining to protocol, which every organization must adopt if it wishes for its traditions to be carried out with dignity and accuracy. Rule one suggests that all protocols be clearly stated in writing so that everyone involved can know what they are and know what to expect. Rule two suggests that a protocol be established for every major function of an organization. Rule three suggests that strict compliance to all matters of protocol be enforced.

When conducting seminars about protocol, or "Standard Operating Procedures" (SOP) (a term I borrowed from my military experience), I am inevitably asked the question, "Is all this really necessary?" I usually respond by insisting that the answer could be either yes or no. Yes, it really is necessary if you want to ensure the orderly conduct of major components of the organization's functions. On the other hand, the answer is no, it is not necessary if it does not matter what the organization looks like when routine functions are done differently each time.

One of the most obvious protocols maintained by religious organizations is that pertaining to vestments: what its officials wear, how its clergy dresses, and when. Of course, other protocols may deal with expense procedures such as how persons are reimbursed, what documents must be turned in, to whom, and when. These are all protocol matters. They are usually designed to ensure timeliness of transactions and fairness in fiduciary matters. In any group, where multiple people operating at different levels of authority are engaged, there must be protocols that govern how persons are placed in such positions, what the levels of authority are, and how persons are handled should problems such as malfeasance, misfeasance, or nonfeasance surface.

Another common area of protocol importance is that of meetings. When meetings are held? How are they to be conducted? What are the protocols for getting things done during the meetings? The list goes on. For years, I was a member of the American Institute of Parliamentarians. As such, not only did I train those wishing to become parliamentarians, but I was also called into organizations to teach parliamentary law to the constituents at large. At other times, I was called into independent organizations to literally conduct their meetings. This was necessitated when major controversy was expected, but the presiding officer was not sufficiently knowledgeable of the protocols of parliamentary law such as Robert's Rules of Order (the major protocol used by churches and other deliberative assemblies). Even though this was an expensive remedy, its cost was well worth the grief that was usually avoided. It was expensive because the average fee for a certified parliamentarian ranged between $1,500 to $2,500 per meeting, in addition to travel costs, hotel accommodations, and per diem.

There are other non-written, and even non-spoken, protocols that are employed during some high-level meetings. For instance, I served as a member of the Board of Bishops of the church organization where I served on the Executive Bishops' Council, the highest ecclesiastical body of the organization. There was an expectation (unspoken protocol) which paired one's right to speak with how long he had served on the board, and his position on the board. I have seen instances where extremely helpful information was ignored because the speaker had "no right" to make such comments due to his lack of tenure on the board.

In church organizations, there are protocols that govern one's eligibility to sit on the rostrum or dais during service events and seating positions. Jesus spoke to the efficacy of such protocol in Luke 14, when He went to share a meal in the home of a leader of the Pharisees. After noticing how guests sought the best seats at the table, He advised them:

> *When someone invites you to a wedding celebration, don't take your seat in the place of honor. Someone more highly regarded than you could have been invited*

by your host. The host who invited both of you will come and say to you, "Give your seat to this other person." Embarrassed, you will take your seat in the least important place. Instead, when you receive an invitation, go and sit in the least important place. When your host approaches you, he will say, "Friend, move up here to a better seat." Then you will be honored in the presence of all your fellow guests. (Luke 14:7–11 CEB)

In addition, there are protocols for how certain people are greeted, and how to address and reply to certain ranks. There are protocols that establish patterns of recognition; protocols exist that suggest the juxtaposition of persons of different ranks as they stand or walk together. If we look closely, we might find a protocol on any involvement in the association with others. While some may not be important in the context of the church or its entities, the church must determine which ones it wishes to adopt. Once adopted, all members are duty-bound to adhere to such protocols.

Church leaders must follow protocol!

Principle 42

Church Leaders Must Be Able to Explain Their Doctrine

But in your hearts revere Christ as Lord. Always be prepared to give an answer to everyone who asks you to give the reason for the hope that you have. But do this with gentleness and respect. —1 Peter 3:15 (NIV)

C hurch leaders often play an influential role among the members of a local church, as well as in the eyes of the general public. Leaders are often seen as voices of the church. It is not uncommon for people to raise questions or concerns to church leaders, as if leaders speak with the authority of the church. Of course, at certain levels of leadership, such leaders do speak with a certain level of authority. No leader will be able to answer all questions raised by members, or the broader community. However, there are some questions that every church leader must be able to answer with ease and conviction: questions of church doctrine, denomination, purpose, core values, etc. All of which should be integrated, to some degree, into the orientation of new members, and especially new leaders. If such information is not offered as part of their orientation, then church leaders must take it upon themselves to seek out the information.

For lay members, this may be viewed as a matter of choice; but for church leaders, being privy to such key information is no longer a matter of choice, but a matter of necessity. It must be regarded as necessary, if for no other reason than to position oneself into a place where he can meet the expectations of the membership and the community at large. In the thinking of some people, religion is religion, and a church is a church. Quite the contrary, there are differences, subtle and otherwise, as people move from denomination to denomination. In fact, one of the great controversies of the non-churched community is the question of such denominational differences. This type of environment breeds questions that church leaders must be able to answer, especially in relationship to their own church. Questions that carry the tone of sincerity must be regarded with sincerity. Obviously, there will be those who, as in the days of Jesus, will ask questions for the purpose of creating conflict; those are to be avoided.

Questions that impact one's ability to make salvific decisions are extremely important. Questions about membership, while important for future evangelistic purposes, may not be as urgent at the time. However, they must still be treated with respect. Statistics show that people often attend multiple churches over an extended period before a decision is made to join. Whatever the question, or the purpose for which the question is asked, Peter admonished the church to *"be ready always to give an answer to every man that asketh you a reason of the hope that is in you with meekness and fear"* (1 Pet. 3:15).

One quality a senior leader looks for when selecting intermediate leaders is the ability to think logically, and to verbalize such thinking in a manner that is logical and coherent. Not only is this necessary for evangelism, but it is helpful for communicating during the normal course of leadership. Another requirement in this area is knowing what to say. A growing trend among many churches is that of selecting leaders from the pool of members whose faithfulness to preaching and teaching services is noted. Possessing a congenial spirit is great, but having the ability to communicate such congeniality in the context of one's doctrinal position is even greater.

To some degree, a church leader is an ambassador of goodwill for the church. As such, leadership must be committed to purposes that closely resemble those of the church. Leadership must reflect the doctrinal position of the church whenever possible. In rare instances where there is a variance between the leader's belief and the doctrine of the church, the leader must be willing to set aside such differences in support of the church's position. In the event such difference is of a nature where it creates a transgression, such leader should humbly resign from the leadership team. In the long run, it is advantageous to have persons in key positions of leadership who are in support of the church as opposed to those who are in opposition to the church. It is imperative that behind the scenes is a spirit of one accord in the church's administration, and on display in all public functions.

Because there may exist the possibility of operational, administrative, or doctrinal conflicts that can be bred and/or fed by either subtle or aggravated—whether intentional or unintentional—disagreements in policies, practices, or doctrine in any church, it is always advisable for the most senior leader to conduct regular meetings with all secondary and intermediate leaders for the sake of promoting a sameness in attitudes, outlook, practices, and ideology among key personnel of the church. Apostle Paul spoke about the problem. He wrote, *"Now I beseech you, brethren, by the name of our Lord Jesus Christ, that ye all speak the same thing, and that there be no divisions among you; but that ye be perfectly joined together in the same mind and in the same judgment"* (1 Corin. 1:10).

Church leaders must be able to explain their doctrine!

Leadership must be committed to purposes that closely resemble those of the church. Leadership must reflect the doctrinal position of the church whenever possible.

Principle 43

Church Leaders Must Extend Grace

Let your speech be alway with grace, seasoned with salt,
that ye may know how ye ought to answer every man.
—Colossians 4:6

More than any other institution, the church is bound by its foundational relationship with God to extend to those who depend upon it for their spiritual well-being, the same proportion of grace shown to every believer. Church members and leaders must not forget that the status enjoyed today by the redeemed was not their status when they first came to Christ. We are not saved because of any self-proclaimed goodness; rather, we are saved because of God's merciful response to our plea for forgiveness. Even our plea of forgiveness was not self-generated; that, too, was an extension of God's grace. In response, God allowed His divine exercise of grace to treat us as if we were fit to stand before His presence. God knew, however, that we were not!

> *For by grace are ye saved through faith; and that not of*
> *yourselves: it is the gift of God: not of works, lest any*
> *man should boast. For we are his workmanship, created*
> *in Christ Jesus unto good works, which God hath be-*
> *fore ordained that we should walk in them.* (Ephesians
> 2:8–10)

I find it amazing when a person's redemptive status appears to be a reflection of his pre-redemption past, as if such person never stood in need of God's unearned forgiving favor. For more than half a century, I have marveled at mankind's capacity to forget who he was, and to replace his past reality with a sanitized version wherein he has always behaved in a godly manner. I have met so many leaders over the years who refused to allow the narratives of their "pre-Christ life" to be known by those whom they lead. Among other sad realities about such person, the saddest is that such refusal negates the glory of God shown upon his life. God's glory does not lie in what you or I have become; instead, God's glory lies in that from which we were transformed. When that narrative is hidden, so then, is the glory of God! Our redemption story must extend unto those whose lives are touched by such redemption. Psalm 107:2 demands that the redeemed share their redemption narrative of the glory of God: *"Let the redeemed of the Lord say so, Whom he hath redeemed from the hand of the enemy...."*

While the sharing of our redemption does indeed include the verbal sharing of such narrative, it also requires us to extend the same manner of grace to those for whom we are responsible. Church leaders must be extremely cautious that they do not become victims of their own selfish pride. It is not uncommon for people who will not share to act as if they have nothing to share. The same principle that Jesus taught in reference to forgiveness applies in the execution of grace. Jesus taught His disciples that when they pray, they are to say, *"Forgive us our trespasses, as we forgive those who trespass against us"* (Matt. 6:12). In other words, forgive us, in the same manner in which we forgive others. It stands to reason that a valid interpretation of such practice is that when we refuse to forgive others, then God is justified in withholding forgiveness from us. Like forgiveness, grace was designed for all mankind. Those who block the flow of grace *from* their lives, in like manner, block the flow of grace *into* their lives. Though spoken in a different context, the words of Paul to the Galatian church rings true in the varying aspects of our actions: *"For whatsoever a man soweth, that shall he also reap"* (Gal. 6:7). Jesus can be heard in Luke's gospel, saying, *"And as ye would that men should do to you, do ye also to them likewise"* (Luke 6:31).

In the performance of our duties as leaders in the church, we must always respond to the failures of others with the same sense of compassion to which Jesus responded to our failures. Paul said to the Roman church, *"For there is no difference...."* God's toleration of the leader's failures is no different from the leader's tolerance of the failures of his followers. Not only does God repeatedly tolerate the shortcomings of those who work in His church, but He forgives such shortcomings as well. Having forgiven such person, God does not hold the offense over his head. This is the same behavior God expects of those who work to serve His church as leaders.

Paul continues his statement of Romans 3:23, *"For there is no difference...,"* by saying in verse 24, *"...for all have sinned, and come short of the glory of God; being justified freely by his grace through the redemption that is in Christ Jesus."*

Just as every leader called of God into church leadership has been justified by faith, so then, has every member who follows. Just as every leader called of God into leadership has peace with God through our Lord Jesus Christ, so then, do the members who follow. Just as every leader called of God into church leadership has access by faith into this grace wherein we stand, so then, does every member who follows. Finally, just as every leader called of God into church leadership rejoices in hope of the glory of God, so then, does every member who follows.

> *Therefore being justified by faith, we have peace with God through our Lord Jesus Christ: by whom also we*

*have access by faith into this grace wherein we stand,
and rejoice in hope of the glory of God.* (Romans 5:1–2)

For the church leader whose personal style of super rigid righteousness makes it difficult to extend to others the grace that God extends to you every day, this is but another area in your life where the transforming grace of God, through Jesus Christ our Lord, is sorely needed. I suggest that you invite God to allow His grace to be spread abroad throughout your heart, and that such grace be bountifully applied to those who look to you for leadership in the Lord's forgiving church.

Church leaders must extend grace!

Principle 44

Church Leaders Must Maintain a Prayer Life

And he spake a parable unto them to this end, that men ought always to pray, and not to faint.   —Luke 18:1

P lease forgive me; I am somewhat embarrassed at the mere thought of suggesting to church leaders that they must maintain a prayer life. Somewhere in this suggestion lies the idea that maybe there are those in this leadership group who need to be reminded of this most fundamental principle. Surely, prayer is a principle that every church leader knows and does on a routine basis. No intelligent leader would dare undertake such tedious effort without the consort of prayer prior to his decision to proceed. But, for the sake of the argument, what could be the harm to church leaders, or, for that matter, to the followers, who do not pray? Could prayer possibly be so important that the failure to pray would result in some negative episode in the lives of those who don't pray?

Let's discuss that for a moment. First, let's explore what prayer does for the individuals who pray frequently and fervently. Prayer serves five primary purposes in the life of a church leader. First, prayer provides for those who pray an opportunity to have fellowship with the most trusted source in life. While such fellowship can serve a variety of purposes, its main purpose is just to "hangout" with God. You need not even have an agenda when you engage in such fellowship. It's like just being in the presence of someone you really like. At times, neither of you have to say anything; just being together is the object of the fellowship. A song we sang as young people in the church expressed this concept better than anything I could say. The song says: "Friendship with Jesus, fellowship divine, Oh, what blessed sweet communion, Jesus is a friend of mine."

Secondly, prayer serves as a vehicle by which your deep appreciation and admiration of God can be expressed without any holds barred. The level of praise directed to God in prayer cannot be equaled through any other method. The wonderful thing about the "expressions of prayer" is that they can be a mixture of talking, crying, yelling, sobbing, joy, frustration, talking fast, not talking at all, ugly faces, rapid modulation of faces, bad grammar, incomplete sentences, talking out of one's head, banging one's head, kneeling, standing, lying, walking, sitting, nodding, even sleeping off and on…. The inexhaustible expressions of prayer! Where else can one be pretty and ugly at the same time? What other time does smart and dumb mix so effortlessly? No other expression allows one to shout at the top of his voice one second, and barely a whisper the next; and the listener is cool?

Thirdly, prayer is a forum in which one can make any petition he wishes to God, from the ridiculous to the sublime. In prayer, there is no risk of anyone being privy to the details of such petition. Our petitions can be made with confidence that God will, in His time, respond. And, somehow, because you made your request to God, the outcome really doesn't matter. Somehow, when you're done, you can walk away with the sense that God heard you, and because God heard you, you have the feeling that everything is going to be alright!

The fourth advantage of a constant prayer exchange with God is that it's therapeutic! As the conscientious leader reflects over the events of the day, often he is besieged with questions. The leader is forced to come face to face with the failures of the day. Did I do it right? Did I do the best I could? Some of the questions that tug at the spirit are even condemning in nature. Did I uphold my faith? Did I walk in the Spirit? Did I say more than I should have said? Was it true, or slightly fabricated? Then comes that soul-crushing question that can stalk the best of us after a long and busy day: Do I need to repent of something I might have said or thought; or, perhaps, a less than charitable way in which I acted? The good news is that prayer can accommodate that need for repentance. Alone at last with God, you can now pour out your soul! Though your heart may be broken, and your soul may feel contrite, your cleansing prayer of forgiveness will surely invoke a forgiving response from God. The psalmist declared: *"The Lord is nigh unto them that are of a broken heart; And saveth such as be of a contrite spirit"* (Psa. 34:18).

Lastly, prayer allows God to talk to you! Those who are in a bad place, where you just need to hear a comforting voice—prayer will do it for you. The sincere leader whose life and work is dedicated to the service of the Lord—I promise you that if you travail long enough, if you cry out to your God sincerely enough, if you shut out life tightly enough … I promise you that at some point during the agony of effectual fervent prayer, God will talk to you. It may not be a long conversation; sometimes it's just a word or a breath of God's presence. Sometimes God simply speaks comfort to a hurting heart; often just a sensation of joy when the burden seems more than you can bear. However God chooses to speak, God does speak! James heard Him speak and encouraged the saints: *"The effectual fervent prayer of a righteous man availeth much"* (Jas. 5:16).

The shame is that those who fail to pray will never enjoy the opportunity to have friendship with Jesus. A prayerless leader will not enjoy the privilege of heaping upon the Lord the unbridled appreciation of a grateful servant; he will miss the ecstasy of expressing his admiration for God. When one does not pray, his petitions are never voiced to God; they go unanswered. The leader who will not pray forfeits the forgiveness of sincere repentance. Perhaps the loneliest feeling ever experienced by man is to live having never felt the presence of God or heard the voice of God speak comfort during the night times of life. Whatever the purpose for which one prays, the comfort of prayer will help you in difficult situations. Prayer grants the courage to fight on. After the five reasons leaders ought to pray, there is a final reason for those who worked in the ditches of life, who carried the burden of leadership in the heat of the day, who travailed for the sake of the saints. They know that if they don't pray, they will faint! Prayer stops the fainting!

Church leaders must maintain a prayer life!

Principle 45

Church Leaders Must Know Their Limitations

*We will not boast about things done outside our area of
authority. We will boast only about what has happened
within the boundaries of the work God has given us, which
includes our working with you. We are not reaching beyond these boundaries when we claim authority over you,
as if we had never visited you ... Nor do we boast and
claim credit for the work someone else has done. Instead,
we hope that your faith will grow so that the boundaries
of our work among you will be extended. Then we will be
able to go and preach the Good News in other places far
beyond you, where no one else is working. Then there will
be no question of our boasting about work done in someone else's territory.* —2 Corinthians 10:13–16 (NLT)

The late Vince Lombardi, an American sports icon whose
team won five National Football League championships, including Super Bowls I and II, and compiled a remarkable
89–29–4 regular season record, was often asked about the success
of his team. One of his most famous replies was, "Teamwork is the
secret that makes common people achieve uncommon results." The
same is true for any effort requiring a joint contribution of multiple people. The church is no exception. If a church is to achieve

its objectives, its people must learn to work together as a team, as opposed to each individual, or groups of individuals, working independently as if they were the whole.

John Maxwell, a noted author and clergyman, wrote a book eighteen years ago titled, *Teamwork Makes the Dream Work!* Maxwell's book is as relevant in today's church as it was then. When the question was raised to more than one hundred pastors of some of America's largest churches, asking what they considered to be the single thing that caused the most controversy within their local churches, the majority of them indicated that it was the inability of church leaders to stay in their lanes. One pastor stated emphatically that too often his leaders "moved about the church as if they were the leaders of the entire church."

This raises two serious questions. The first question is: What is there about the culture of the church that energizes a leader to the point that he feels he is in charge? The second question is: What is going on in the psyche of such a leader that makes him feel he is in charge?

The size of any local church, or church organization, often determines whether secondary and intermediate leaders are salaried, or work on a voluntary basis. In either case, it is difficult to find qualified leaders whose personal chemistry flows with the culture of a particular church. As many senior church leaders can attest, finding the right leadership personality is one of the most time-consuming efforts with the least value-ratio that most leaders are asked to perform. This is due, in part, because after months of searching and interviewing candidates for a position, once the decision is made to hire a particular candidate, and acclimate him to the culture of the church, he often resigns before the value of the time spent in the hiring process is realized. It appears that the turnover of paid leadership staff in medium to large churches is far greater than most people imagine. I have interviewed several pastors who indicated that it is such a draining exercise that they dread the process. Some stated that when that process is completed, then comes the tedious, but often failed effort of securing a long-term commitment from such person. Several senior pastors expressed very candidly that their "new leadership hires" would come in with attitudes that suggested that the church did little to nothing before they got there.

My observation has been that in some churches, there was such an "air of desperation" for human resources that the administrative staff gave off signals that gave birth to the highly egocentric behavior seen in some of the newly acquired leadership staff. It is one thing to welcome new staff, but an altogether different thing to make such person feel as if he is the "savior" of the church. One pastor made a remark that "when a person is treated in such a kingly manner, he becomes the king!" While we want to welcome new staff in an "inviting manner," we don't want to give the impression that we could not exist without them. I advise pastors and church administrators to set firm ground rules for the engagement of all new staff so that the assumed "privilege of having" is transformed into a "privilege of being." In other words, rather than a new staff member feeling like "they ought to be happy to have me," he will be made to feel "happy to be there."

The question of whether it is better to appoint people from within the church to available leadership positions, or to hire people from the outside to fill such positions, is still a very hotly debated issue. I cannot certify one above the other; I have witnessed the good, the bad, and the ugly of both sides of the issue. This is a determination that would be best made by the local entity involved.

The second of the two questions is: What's going on in the psyche of such leaders that make them feel as if they are in charge? In general, a vast majority of candidates applying for leadership positions have psychological profiles that overlap on both the aggressive, self-motivated, goal-oriented, extroverted personality, and the attentive, humble, "following orders" type personality. Being a successful leader requires a very delicate balance in the psychological makeup of such a person. Due to the complexities of the balancing requirements, it is very easy to slip to one side over the other as such leader navigates the thin margins of each. The sad reality is that given the prestige involved in most church leadership positions, and the uniqueness of the necessary characteristics of those filling such positions, the equation sometimes lends itself to the development of egomaniacal personalities.

Very rarely does one find a leadership personality that is totally submissive and malleable to the pre-existent culture of any church or church organization. I am not suggesting that it is not possible, but it is, indeed, very, very rare. It is, however, one of those areas of the human personality that must yield to the influence of the Holy Spirit if such leader is to maximize his potential in a church leadership role. There are several personality adaptations that must take place. For instance, the natural curiosity of an aggressive personality is that he will often reach over into the next area when he senses a need for intervention. While in some arenas, this might be helpful; in others, this could be very disturbing. It is even more disturbing when the leader of the other area is just as aggressive and attentive as the leader who reaches over to help. While church leaders should be available to assist each other in the accomplishment of the ultimate objective—the successful operation of the mission of the church—such assistance must be offered in a manner that does not infringe upon the leadership prerogative of one's fellow leader, or that of any senior leader. At any rate, church leaders must learn to stay in their lane; must learn to engage themselves exclusively in the area of their function; must learn to respond only when asked; or must learn to ask if they can intervene prior to doing so.

Church leaders must know their limitations!

Principle 46

Church Leaders Must Be Led by the Spirit

For as many as are led by the Spirit of God, they are the sons of God. —Romans 8:14

In the culture of today's church, it is very easy to be led off track by the many independent concerns that beckon day and night for the leader's attention. Such aggressive beckoning can become quite enticing if the leader is not extremely careful as he goes about the delicate business of his routine leadership tasks. Because many church leaders are multi-faceted, it is not uncommon for them to have interests and skills in multiple areas of endeavor. That is, in part, what makes them such good leaders! The sad reality, however, is that the very thing that often serves to the advantage of such leaders can, if not properly monitored, serve to his destruction as well. Active curiosity is often the product of an above average intelligence. This results in a propensity to explore many areas of distraction. Obviously, the more exploration one becomes involved in, the greater the risk that he will be sucked into some of those interests.

Please allow me to affirm unconditionally that the intellectual capacity to multitask must in no way be considered a negative characteristic of those gifted in such ways. My only concern is in making sure that such persons understand the responsibility to guard against the tendency to become over productive in the areas of distractions, while being grossly under productive in other areas. All too often, the under productive area is, in fact, his main area of responsibility. There is a great deal of truth to the adage that busy people often become too busy for their own good. This usually happens when secondary activities interfere with primary activities to the degree that such interference erodes the effectiveness necessary for success in one's main responsibility.

Another area of grave concern for church leaders who operate from the position of higher-than-average intellectual capacity is that of being pushed by too many voices. By voices, I am referring to such driving forces as inner urges, ideas, and dreams. Urges, for instance, are often defined as the impulses that compel us to act; without which, some things, both necessary and unnecessary, would be left undone. In many ways, one's everyday behavior is characterized by urges that push him to act. In a similar manner, dreams often inspire a leader to push past what he customarily does. To some, dreams provide a sense of purpose and/or direction. In addition, they often serve as motivators as well. Likewise, ideas transform one's perception of what is possible, while inspiring him to push forward. Ideas can generate even more power as they shape meaning.

Primary tasks or secondary functions, ideas, dreams, and inner urgings—all of these, and many more motivating factors are necessary to supply both the energy and the commitment to move forward during times of melancholy or discouragement. Often, the excitement of other activities supplies the subtle nudge that keeps the engines of duty running. As church leaders visualize and understand their mission, and, as such mission is conceptualized into the prize for which one works, the risk of being sidetracked becomes less probable. Leaders can glean a sense of the importance of being fixed on their objective from the writing of Isaiah to whom God spoke in Isaiah 45:22:

Principle 46: Must Be Led by the Spirit

Look unto me, and be ye saved, all the ends of the earth:
for I am God, and there is none else.

To "look," in this text, is not merely a momentary glance or casual notice; but rather, it means to stare, to gaze, to fix one's eyes upon. God is imploring Israel to fix their eyes on Him to the point that they stare with an exclusivity that blocks out anyone else or anything else that could otherwise distort their vision or obscure their objective. One must take on the attitude as expressed in the classic song from the late 1950s by a group known as the Flamingos; they sang, "I only have eyes for you!" That means, no matter what the intended distraction might be, I only have eyes for you; no matter how beautiful the other person is, I only have eyes for you.

When church leaders approach their assignment with the kind of focus that God admonished Israel to employ, their function will not be altered, nor their vision obscured. I submit that this is an easy challenge to those who make their calling and election sure. For this, I refer to 2 Peter 1:10, where he urged the church: *"Wherefore the rather, brethren, give diligence to make your calling and election sure: for if ye do these things, ye shall never fall."* Such diligence assures leaders, whose calling and election are certain, that they cannot fail. It also fulfills the second half of Romans 8:14, where Paul reminds the church who the real sons of God are. He said, *"For as many as are led by the Spirit of God, they are the sons of God."*

As long as church leaders, regardless of the level of such leadership, whether one leads in the local church, the national church, or a supporting agency of the church—as long as you are one of the sons of God, you will inherently be led by the Spirit of God! I implore all functional church leaders to make this their number one priority. Not only does your success as a church leader depend on it, but also, your success as a man or woman of God is wholly hinged upon how well this task is executed.

Church leaders must be led by the Spirit!

Principle 47

Church Leaders Must Not Be Given to Gossip

But shun profane and vain babblings: for they will increase unto more ungodliness.   —2 Timothy 2:16

Some time ago I made note of one of the best quotes I had ever read about gossip. While I do not remember the author, I trust that my memory of the quote will sufficiently convey the spirit intended by the author: "Refusing to gossip is a beautiful decision to make. It not only creates richer friendships but, more importantly, it makes our relationship with the Lord more authentic and believable. We honor God when we honor each other."

Gossip is defined as casual or unconstrained conversation or reports, most often of a derogatory nature, about other people, typically involving details that are not confirmed as being true. I have often wondered what those who gossip get from such activity. Insight Therapy, LLC, an outpatient mental health practice that treats both gossipers and victims of gossip, was asked, "So, why do people gossip?" Their answer was:

> As social creatures, we're hard-wired for connection. And, sometimes, gossip can provide us with a sense of bonding that we all lure, regardless of whether the conversation is positive or negative. Some experts

view gossip as evidence of cultural learning, wherein we learn what's socially acceptable and what's not. For example, if someone lies frequently and people start talking about that person negatively, the collective criticism is intended to warn others of the consequences of lying. Generally speaking, most gossip falls into the "negative" category.

People gossip for a variety of reasons:

To feel superior. Many people who feel insecure about themselves find temporary relief in judging others. Knowing something that others don't can feel empowering, and sometimes, that's all an uncertain gossiper needs. But it can also make you appear untrustworthy.

They have a sadistic personality. Emotional sadism—someone who comes off as harsh, aggressive, intimidating, or demeaning is rooted in gossip. This type of character enjoys knowing that someone else is experiencing pain or misfortune; delighted it's not happening to them.

They're bored. When people can't generate exciting discussions based on knowledge or ideas, gossip can arouse people's interest.

Anxiety. According to research, anxious people are more likely to spread rumors and partake in gossip. And since uncertainty, or feeling out of control, is significant in anxiety, gossiping can make such person get that sense of control back.

<u>To feel like part of the group</u>. Alongside that feeling of connection we desire, sometimes people gossip to feel like they belong to the group. Being the center of someone or a group's attention while gossiping can be compared to buying attention. Yet, this feeling of acceptance isn't based on a person's identity or personality, but exclusion or maliciousness.[7]

Although Insight Therapy did not address one of my major concerns about gossip—especially when such behavior is coming from someone who occupies a position of influence and authority—which is that gossiping may cause one's followers to lose respect for their leader out of the fear that they may themselves become the next victim. This can become even more alarming when a follower is aware that his leader is privy to damaging information about him. And while a large percentage of gossip consists of information not confirmed by the gossiper, most therapists agree that even gossip that is based on truth can still cause negative consequences for all involved.

Church leaders must subscribe to Paul's philosophy: *"For I determined not to know anything among you, save Jesus Christ, and him crucified"* (1 Corin. 2:2). Paul's motive was to assuage their apprehensions regarding his preaching; he took this opportunity to address the "elephant in the room." He is saying, even though *"I was with you in weakness, and in fear, and in much trembling,"* you need not worry about me using my knowledge of your personal problems to gossip about you to others.

Followers need to know that they are protected from malicious gossip and other social weapons of attack. A prudent leader can address that very real, but unspoken, concern in two ways. First,

---

7   Blog Article #137, (2020). Why People Gossip and How You Can Cope. Insight Therapy, LLC

he can assure them, as Paul did, of his leadership principles concerning such matters. Next, he can practice what he preaches. The last thing a sincere leader wishes is to be caught in a vicious cycle of distrust; this quickly minimizes the ability to lead. Solomon advised "members" not to hang out with gossipers: *"He that goeth about as a talebearer revealeth secrets: Therefore meddle not with him that flattereth with his lips"* (Prov. 20:19).

Solomon also advised "church leaders" against sharing people's secrets: *"When arguing with your neighbor, don't betray another person's secret. Others may accuse you of gossip, and you will never regain your good reputation"* (Prov. 25:9–10 NLT).

Gossiping appears to be harmless on the surface, but it is one of the most destructive behavioral patterns in which a leader can, with little to no effort, become ensnared. Any leader who finds himself involved in the affairs of others in such a way that can be misconstrued as gossip, must move resolutely to end such involvement. A leader must understand that he should be committed to the well-being of his followers, and the overall spiritual and social health of the church. Even more important is the realization that he is responsible to God for all aspects of his conduct. A leader must realize that words, actions, and reactions all contribute to his success, or lack thereof. As does anyone responsible for the well-being of others, a leader wants to feel that he made a positive contribution in the lives of his followers.

Church leaders must not be given to gossip!

Principle 48

Church Leaders Must Remain in Fellowship with God

God is faithful, by whom ye were called unto the fellowship of his Son Jesus Christ our Lord.
                                                    —1 Corinthians 1:9

Fellowship can be defined as the joining together of separate entities, thus making them one in purpose. Such fellowship between God and man is brought about by salvation, which is God's process of redeeming those who are otherwise lost. This brings mankind together with God, and creates a viable fellowship between the two, a union that will last until one of those in fellowship moves to sever the union. The wonderful thing about fellowship with God is that He never seeks to sever His fellowship with any person to whom He is joined. If one's fellowship with God is broken, it is because of actions taken on the part of the person; it was certainly not God who broke the fellowship. Fellowship with God can only be broken by sin for which one fails to repent! I can attest to that because of the extensive effort orchestrated by God to initiate the fellowship. At no point can the sacrifice of Jesus Christ for the sins of a lost world be deemed frivolous. In fact, in circumstances where one lives in ways that appear as if he wishes to terminate his fellowship with God, he will find that God does not give up easily.

It is needful to remind the church that God does not enjoy the way-wardness of His children. He does not rejoice in the commission of sin by those whom He has redeemed. God does not see the occasion of sin in the life of a believer as an excuse to "zap" him with His "radar gun" of sovereign righteousness. God is not like the traffic cop who lies in wait behind a sign with his radar gun pointed at clueless drivers. That idea suggests some kind of "benefit" on the part of the enforcer. To the contrary, God does not set "sin traps" or stings. God does not find pleasure in the failure of His children. God gets no "divine benefit" when those for whom He died commit sin.

God does not accept, rejoice in, nor benefit from the sins of the saints. Another of God's assuring attributes is that He does not give up on us easily. With God, unlike behavior displayed by some church leaders, there are no "throw-away" saints whose membership is no longer welcomed because they acted in a way that was against the rules. Make no mistake about it; God cannot overlook our sins any more than He accepts them. Before one commits an act of sin, or puts himself into a position of sin, the Holy Spirit responds in an effort to preclude any breach in the union of the redeemed and the redeemer. If, however, the leading of the Holy Spirit goes unheeded, and sin is consummated, God moves to bring about a "condemning awareness" that is designed to bring the offending party into condemnation. God's purpose in such condemnation is to bring the person to repentance so that He can have an opportunity to exercise His mercy and forgive the sin of such person. As sin breaks our fellowship with God, repentance restores our fellowship with God.

How can a church leader be out of fellowship with God? I suggest that one possibility may be that the leader is guilty of not following the guidance of the Holy Spirit. The greatest benefit of having access to the Spirit is the guidance received from the Spirit.

Principle 48: Must Remain in Fellowship with God

If guidance is to prove beneficial, we must learn to follow it precisely. What value is there to having instructions for completing a complex project if we decide not to follow them? You will end up either with a botched project or a frustrated project manager. Such unwanted results could have been avoided if we had respected and adhered to the instructions. A church leader who refuses to be guided by the instructions of the Holy Spirit will end up frustrated while bringing confusion upon the group that he is charged with leading.

Another possibility, and a great contributor to the sins of the redeemed, is little knowledge, or a blatant lack of knowledge, of the Word of God. I contend that any failure by the average church leader results from mistakes due to the level to which he knows the Word of God. The noun form of the word "mistake" is defined as "an error or fault; a misconception or misunderstanding." In the verb form, mistake is defined as "to understand wrongly; misinterpret, to recognize or identify incorrectly; to err."

I contend that the sins of the redeemed are not usually the result of a lack of love for God, nor any disregard for that which pleases God. The average church leader wishes to please God more than anything; he simply does not know how to please God. Those who wrestle with a lack of knowledge must start with a commitment to get to know God better through regular communication with God by way of the ministry of prayer and daily Bible reading.

While pleasing God must always lie at the center of the heart of a church leader, it must never become a badge of pride. Pleasing God benefits the leader more than God. When a leader routinely makes God happy—which is a result of a lifestyle of operating within God's pleasure—the incidence of sin in the life of such God-pleasing leader diminishes significantly. The more adamant one becomes about the conduct of godliness in his daily affairs, the less effort he will spend in pursuit of a sinless existence with

God. A church leader is able to minimize his efforts of avoiding sin, while maximizing the effects of enjoying the blessings of the "perfect peace" promised by God to those whose mind is stayed on Him. Perfect peace can be described as peace without the interruption of sin. A leader who attains that peaceful state of life will prove himself to be a church leader extraordinaire, as he becomes equally extraordinary as a person. His new extraordinary status will be readily visible in every position held in life. He will become a decisively better parent, a better offspring, a better spouse, a better sibling, a better relative, a better friend, a better church member, and, of course, a better church leader.

Church leaders must remain in fellowship with God!

Principle 49

Church Leaders Must Not Serve the Flesh

There is therefore now no condemnation to them which are in Christ Jesus, who walk not after the flesh, but after the Spirit. —Romans 8:1

There is a great dichotomy between living according to the desires of the Spirit as opposed to living out the wishes of one's flesh. Not only are those two factors different, but they also move in opposite directions. They are entirely opposed to each other without any possibility of ever being reconciled. The two ends are now, and will always be, at odds with one another. Paul speaks rather strongly about this problem as it visibly existed in the church at Rome. It is to be greatly appreciated that in the Roman church there operated a leader who had the strength of character to confront the misguided communion of the Spirit and the flesh. A critical misappropriation in today's church is the tendency among some leaders to treat the Spirit and flesh as if they were willing companions, working together towards the same end. Quite the contrary, our flesh carries the baggage of perilous condemnation, whereas the Spirit lives freely within the fellowship of Jesus Christ. What a distinct dichotomy!

As we explore the theology of Paul, as taught in Romans 8, the separation between the Spirit and the flesh becomes abundantly clear.

Leaders who attempt to live according to the desires of the flesh are primarily involved in matters that categorically enhance the flesh. By contrast, those whose interest is in operating in a manner that pleases the Spirit are committed to a way of life that amplifies and strengthens the Spirit. The two directions are incompatible. We cannot travel on the highway of the flesh and arrive at a strong spiritually directed life. Neither do we travel on the route of the Spirit and end up in a place of condemnation.

> *For they that are after the flesh do mind the things of the flesh; but they that are after the Spirit the things of the Spirit.* (Rom. 8:5)

While I would like to say that there appears to have been a mass amalgamation of the flesh and Spirit over the past forty to fifty years, as evidenced by Paul's writings, this undercurrent of betrayal has been brewing in the church for many years. The crucial challenge of today's church is to find leaders whose courage affords them the strength to redirect this anomaly. Leaders must accept the reality that Satan's most concerted mission has been to supplant the element of spiritual mindedness with a strong attitude of carnality. Just as the Roman government inserted into the administration of the church men who were more politician than they were churchmen, and were consequentially more successful in politicizing the church to the point that it no longer represented Christ, Satan has employed the same tactics in his attempt to undermine the Spirit of God in today's church and replace it with carnal-minded leaders. As such, the church has been besieged by leaders whose primary interest is the promotion of self. One of my most esteemed colleagues put it this way, "The ministry of the church has gone from building the kingdom of God to building palaces for themselves." Somewhere along the way, we forgot Paul's admonition of verses 7 and 8: *"Because the carnal mind is enmity against God: for it is not subject to the law of God, neither indeed can be. So then they that are in the flesh cannot please God."*

Somehow the church must seek to put in place a cadre of leaders who, while still *of* the flesh—the human status of all mankind until the time of the rapture—are not *in* the flesh, but in the Spirit. For such leaders, it is apparent that the Spirit of God dwells within. Every leader in today's church must come to grips with both his intentions and continued commitment. The question must be answered repeatedly: "Whose servant am I?" For those who cannot answer such question unequivocally, my advice is to either resign from your position of church leader, despite the level at which you work; or, to allow an infusion of the Holy Spirit to transform you into the type of leader God has called you to be. Anything short of the latter is not only a detriment to the church, but it is a death sentence upon the leader. Paul emphasized the same choices and results quite dramatically; he declared in verse 13: *"For if ye live after the flesh, ye shall die: but if ye through the Spirit do mortify the deeds of the body, ye shall live."*

The church is in a most vulnerable position at this stage of its existence; the caliber of leadership that embraces the church from this day forward will either enhance its ministry or inflict great harm upon its effectiveness. I would not want to be among the leaders of the church whose deliberate denial of purpose and performance causes God to spew his vengeance upon such leaders. Just as God responded to such deviant behavior in the Old Testament, the God of the New Testament will respond in kind upon today's leaders. God said in 2 Chronicles 7:14: *"If my people, which are called by my name, shall humble themselves, and pray, and seek my face, and turn from their wicked ways; then will I hear from heaven, and will forgive their sin, and will heal their land."*

The irony is that as one who commits himself to God, the church leader will be more personally enhanced than he could ever be while living opposed to God's requirements. God has always taken care of those who follow after Him! The pattern of God's commitment to His people has remained unquestionable throughout all generations. The psalmist said it best when he said: *"I have been young, and now am old; Yet have I not seen the righteous forsaken, nor his seed begging bread"* (Psa. 37:25).

Church leaders must not serve the flesh!

Principle 50

Church Leaders Must Not Operate in Fear

*For God hath not given us the spirit of fear; but of power,
and of love, and of a sound mind.* —2 Timothy 1:7

Fear has no place in the thinking or actions of God-centered church leaders! Fear has been known to cause debilitating paralysis at moments of decisions that are most crucial to the mission of the church. I have helplessly watched a thriving church lose its most needed momentum that took years to develop because of fear of making what most leaders would view as a simple decision. Fear is almost always the result of either the loss of faith or, at best, the retardation of one's faith. The problem in both instances is that fear gives the adversary a brief advantage by allowing pauses of movement that break the progression that rallies support. Fear often throws necessary timing out of whack. Even though an event might be within its season in the life of a church, timing is essential to every season. That is the essence of the writing of Ecclesiastes: *"To every thing there is a season, and a time to every purpose under the heaven.... I said in mine heart, God shall judge the righteous and the wicked: for there is a time there for every purpose and for every work"* (Eccl. 3:1, 17).

Apostle Paul made two observations about fear that should be comforting to biblically-minded church leaders. He assured the Roman church that they live under the care and protective cover of a loving Father who holds the reins of their universe. *"For ye have not received the spirit of bondage again to fear; but ye have received the Spirit of adoption, whereby we cry, Abba, Father"* (Rom. 8:15).

The use of the phrase *"Abba, Father"* is translated in the Good News Bible as *"Father, my Father"*! Our adoption into the sonship of God gives us the privilege to call on Him as a *"very present help in the time of trouble."* Paul denotes that fear is the enslavement of bondage. But the words of Jesus in John 8:36 remind us: *"If the Son therefore shall make you free, ye shall be free indeed."* An active relationship with Jesus Christ is our guarantee that we are no longer subjected to the bondage from which His grace—His unmerited favor—has delivered us. Jesus said, *"He that followeth me shall not walk in darkness, but shall have the light of life"* (John 8:12).

Paul's second observation concerning fear that should be of comfort to church leaders today, as during the time of Paul's writing, is that God replaces the spirit of fear with a spirit of power, a spirit of love, and a spirit of sound-mindedness. *"For God hath not given us the spirit of fear; but of power, and of love, and of a sound mind"* (2 Tim. 1:7).

These three advantages, wholly reserved for those who, in obedience, respect the sovereignty of God, will easily overcome Satan-inspired destructive fear. I cringe when I see church leaders operating in a spirit of fear instead of from the vantage point of power, love, and sound mind. In the long run, fear causes weakness and erratic thinking! There is no leadership in weakness or the instability of erratic thinking; such deterrence can only lead to defeat. Godly leadership, on the other hand, is never effective during moments of defeat; positive leadership thrives in the arena of God-directed decisiveness!

One of the most important things that one must always remember about fear is that it is an emotion. And, like any emotion, it is often based on one's perception rather than one's reality. Church leaders cannot afford the instability of acting on emotions or mere perceptions; church leaders can better serve their followers by demonstrating the kind of stability that is devoid of fear. Many years ago, I heard the Reverend Billy Graham make one of the most profound statements I have ever heard regarding the management of fear. He said, "When fear knocks at your door, send faith to answer; you will find no one there!" He was, in contrast, juxtaposing fear with faith. What Graham was saying, in essence, was that faith and fear cannot both exist at the same time; the presence of one automatically dismisses the other. While there are times when fear can be classified as a legitimate precaution, it is, however, never intended to displace our faith. Faith, on the other hand, can always dislodge our fears, even when such fears are legitimate. The result of faith over fear will always prove beneficial to both leader and member.

Another word for fear is the word "phobia," the nuance of which speaks to the degree of one's fear. While phobia does denote an extreme or irrational fear, some social scientists regard all fear as irrational, or, at least, the resulting actions of all fear. Those who work in fear management will often advise the victims of fear to employ one of two strategies: fight it or avoid it. To fight fear is to challenge the cause of fear. For instance, the person who is afraid to fly is advised to compare the risk of flying (the number of injuries and of deaths associated with in-flight accidents) to the risks of other modes of transportation. While the numbers differ from agency to agency, it is generally agreed that there is one automobile fatality per every five in-flight fatalities. That statistic alone suggests that being an automobile passenger is five times more dangerous than being an airline passenger.

The other strategy for fear is to avoid it. To avoid fear is to alter one's life to the degree that areas that cause fear must be avoided as much as possible. Of course, this could result in a tremendous loss of time and opportunity for the average person. The question raised by this method is: Is it worth the effort? My question to church leaders is: Why expend the unnecessary time and effort avoiding something that is only a perception at best? Furthermore, why not learn to utilize the resources intrinsic in the life of a Spirit-filled leader, as opposed to reacting to something that may very well be aggravated beyond reality? Reacting to fear in this manner is a real possibility that all believers must guard against as they walk in faith. Church leaders must take care to ensure that their actions encourage followers in their faith walk, as opposed to passively pandering to their fears.

Church leaders must not operate in fear!

Principle 51

Church Leaders Must Have a Testimony

*And they overcame him by the blood of the Lamb, and by
the word of their testimony; and they loved not their lives
unto the death.* —Revelation 12:11

For many churchgoers around the world, a testimony is a personal account of an experience in the life of such person, usually sharing an experience with God, or some element of the church in the life of such person. To put it succinctly, a testimony is a "this is what God did for me moment"; it is often unsolicited and very believable for the listeners. In ways, personal testimonies solidify the claims of the church in the minds and hearts of those who may or may not be a part of the church. It represents first-hand knowledge!

I find it ironic that, for many years, business organizations, non-profit institutions, educational communities, and almost every type of public and private entity have capitalized extensively using personal testimonies. Advertising agencies have resorted to the use of testimonies in the solicitation of patronage for products from A to Z. It is difficult to turn on the television without being bombarded by ads commercializing testimonials on the use of a plethora of products and services. Testimonials are now a way of doing business in both public and private social media. Such advertisements are not always in good taste, but someone is always willing to give their testimony attesting to the virtue of products and services.

I recall that during my last trip to Africa, I spent a day or two in Amsterdam. After checking into an upscale brand hotel, I turned the television on during a commercial in which someone was extolling the virtues of a particular "house of prostitution" and the women employed there. It was obvious that prostitution was legal in the Netherlands. During that visit, I also heard television commercials featuring testimonials about marijuana and other unpleasant things. The truth is that testimonies work!

However, in recent years the church seems to have gotten away from the ritual of "testimony services" during both Sunday and midweek services where individuals would stand and give voice to anything that represented a positive experience with God. Such experiences could be based on things that happened at work, school, in the neighborhood, or just in life in general. Such experience did not always speak about the church, or anyone in the church; rather, it usually spoke to some life victory that resulted from one's relationship with Jesus Christ.

One would be utterly amazed at how effective such brief testimonies were in the day-to-day lives of those who were struggling to maintain a sense of commitment to the things of God. As a man in my mid-seventies, I retain vivid memories of many of the testimonies I heard during my youth. I can't adequately express how much my life in Christ was helped by those testimonies. Today, as I travel around the country ministering in churches of varying denominations, to people of varying backgrounds, I hardly ever hear of the "testimonial services" of my youth. I do not make the following statement as a case in fact; however, I firmly believe that the pervasive lack of commitment that plagues church members today is due, in part, to the lack of such testimonies. Contrary to the thoughts of some senior church leaders, members need to hear the victory experiences that flow from testimony to testimony. The sense of victory one gets from the testimonies of others is indispensable to those who struggle with some of the same complexities of life.

Members who wish to live up to the highest level of their spiritual potential must realize that God placed in us the capacity to live victoriously. As victory is a hallmark of godly living, the sharing of such victory in testimony is suggestive of the same victory for others! It is important to God that church leaders and members share the testimonies of their victorious living for the following reasons:

1. Testimonies assist in assuring a better experience!

2. Testimonies demonstrate adequate care!

3. Testimonies promote the praise of God!

Testimonies assist in assuring a better experience!

One of the responsibilities, and privileges, Christ left to His church was that of sharing the stories of trials and victories. Testifying is an intrinsic part of the victory of sharing faith experiences with those struggling with similar encounters. It is a valuable tool for maintaining the spiritual growth of those in the church. The activity of testifying is inclusive of all elements of one's life. Such verbal communications are most essential to the process of testifying, as are all aspects of a believer's life. Whereas personal testimonies are most important to our stories, so are our actions. Other important factors are things such as our reactions to the unexpected, how we handle life's adversities, and our attitudes about life. All actions and reactions of life affect our capacity for successful living. These are all elements of our testimony—testimonies that are the responsibility of every member and leader!

The question is not: Must church leaders testify of the goodness of Christ? Rather, the question is: What kind of testimony must church leaders become? It is as imperative now as ever in the history of the church that we understand the unique relationship between testimonies and growth. It is without question that the strength of our testimony will affect our growth. The more excited we are about the message of our testimony, the more effective we are as leaders. We must realize that a testimony is more effective when it comes from a posture of one's personal experience.

No one is helped by what appears to be a helplessly sad, drab testimony, or by a testimony that paints a portrait of a life hopelessly surrounded by pain and melancholy. The atmosphere of our testimony is as important as the content of our testimony. The three "Cs" of testifying are character, context, and content. A negative position for either of these factors could destroy the effectiveness of the remaining two and destroy a potential relationship with Jesus Christ! Character speaks to the lifestyle of the person testifying; context speaks to the attitude and disposition of the person testifying; finally, content speaks to the message of the testimony. While monitoring the styles and techniques of those engaged in the testifying process, it has become clear that a victorious life and a victorious attitude almost always result in a successful testimonial experience. The content becomes a positive affirmation of lifestyle and disposition. And, while not many members will be helped without such positive confirmation, it must never be regarded as the sum total of the testimony! Again, a victorious lifestyle and a victorious testimony are a must!

Another indispensable benefit of the testimony is that it demonstrates sincerity. Effective leadership must bear definitive evidence of sincerity, the aura of which must be conveyed to the members that we attempt to lead. In order for leadership to enjoy the necessary ingredient of sincerity, it must have an experiential object upon which to be based. Sustained leadership cannot be based solely upon what someone else saw or experienced; a good leader must have a testimony based upon his own interactions with life!

Testimonies demonstrate adequate care!

In addition to assuring a better experience, testimonies show the care of God for His people! When I was young, my father often sang a song that spoke to God's continued care. It stated over and over: *"Jesus, I'll never forget what You've done for me; Jesus, I'll never forget how You set me free; Jesus, I'll never forget how You brought me out; Jesus, I'll never forget, no, never!"* At the risk of a philosophical argument with those who subscribe to the belief that we can do anything we set our minds to, I'd like to suggest that while we can do many things to contain some of life's difficulties, there comes a point when the only power that can help us is the power of God!

Contrary to the belief of those who subscribe to Abraham Maslow's "hierarchy of needs," man is not self-sufficient! The Bible admonishes us to be strong; the divine modifier is that we *"be strong in the Lord, and in the power of his might"* (Eph. 6:10). We are to be strong, but we must always recognize that our strength is in the Lord. A tool Satan uses against us is the deceit of making us feel that we can function in our own strength. Somehow, he makes us feel we are self-sufficient! Nothing could be further from the truth. Our testimony is in the power of God's might! Apostle Paul advised the saints at Ephesus that *"we wrestle not against flesh and blood, but against principalities, against powers, against the rulers of the darkness of this world, against spiritual wickedness in high places"* (Eph. 6:12).

This kind of fighting requires a capacity far beyond any inherent ability that lies in our heredity. Genetic qualities transferred at birth may predispose an offspring to certain characteristics that, when properly nurtured, may result in a greater inclination for strategic thinking; but that is not enough to handle life's problems as we fight against the wiles of Satan. Fighting against principalities, powers, rulers of darkness, and spiritual wickedness requires much more than what we learn through the socialization process. This kind of fighting requires a capacity that can only be realized through the power of God! Because it is important to God that His children have a testimony, He supplies us with all necessary strength!

The theology of my childhood church reinforced, through song and testimony, the principles of God's care. Many of the verses echoed during the testimony services, "Be not dismayed whate'er betide, God will take care of you! Beneath His wings of love abide, God will take care of you!" We gleaned from such testimonies a confidence that superseded any fragment of doubt that might have been thrown into our midst, a confidence that armed us with the faith that whatever we face in life, we do not face it alone. We were assured God was with us, and in all circumstances, we would emerge as victors. The theology of our pastor was shaped by his experiences of trial and victory. He testified that God always met him at the point of need!

Emerging from a life made up of victory after victory, it is not difficult to find a genuine testimony whelming up in one's spirit. Victory produces a testimony, especially when one realizes that victory is the result of a power greater than oneself. Growing up in a small church, I often heard such assurances. We were assured and reassured that God was with us. Testimony service was consumed by texts and slogans affirming the belief that God was on our side.

It quickly became apparent to all of us that our testimony was indeed beneficial; it demonstrated the providence of God in the care of His people. As much as we wanted to have victory, God wanted it for us more. Victory makes our testimony easy; it is proof of God's care for us! That is why Satan actively seeks to strip us of any testimonies of past victories. We must guard those sacred memories by rehearsing them, as God instructed Israel, to our children, our children's children, and throughout all generations.

Testimonies promote the praise of God!

In addition to assuring a better experience and showing adequate care, our testimonies show forth our praise of God! In his letter to the church at Rome, Apostle Paul, in Romans 1:17, asserts, *"For therein is the righteousness of God revealed from faith to faith...."* In like manner, the flames of our testimony are fanned from faith to faith. Another depiction of Paul's meaning could be "from faith experience to faith experience!" As church leaders, every victory must result in a testimony that strengthens the people of God. For members who struggle in the faith, the mere testimony of past victory brings joy. The excitement of victory cannot resist the expressions of praise when it is shared in a powerful testimony! It is imperative that leaders share their personal testimonies of winning against the personal attacks of Satan in their day-to-day affairs! In the meantime, God loves the testimony of His children. God knows that victory produces a testimony, and a testimony produces praise!

Church leaders must have a testimony!

The more excited we are about the message of our testimony, the more effective we are as leaders.

Principle 52

Church Leaders Must Practice "Real Praise"

Let every thing that hath breath Praise the Lord. Praise ye the Lord. —Psalm 150:6

A critical change that began during the mid-twentieth century has taken place in the church. It has been labeled by Pentecostals and some other Evangelicals as a "praise explosion!" From the surface it appears to have the effect of unifying the church around the activity of worship in the expression of audible, physical, and emotional praise. Many Christians have become far more vocal in their worship than at any other time in the history of the church since the Dark Ages and Reformation. It appears that the stigma of shame that was once attached to people involved in Christianity has evolved into a proud assertion of godly status. The social stigma that at one time followed those who dared to publicly declare themselves Christians has been lifted by the overwhelming percentage of modern-day churchgoers who label themselves as such. In addition, the fear of being labeled as radical because of extreme emotional displays has evolved into a kind of "pride of belonging."

Be it right-wing conservative evangelicals or left-wing liberals, the term "Christian" has become a universal rallying cry which denotes an active relationship with Jesus Christ! This state of belonging is accompanied by all the emotional activity displayed by Christians today. It is no longer viewed as negative behavior to lift our voices during the earnestness of worship to the level of a shout in a public display of praise. This highly emotional, and often intense, personal act of public worship is generally greeted with enthusiasm by fellow worshipers. While such emotional display often invokes the same kind of response from others, it can be the expression of a single person in a crowd of hundreds and still be acceptable. This kind of worship may be the result of something intensely personal in the life of the individual worshiper; but the excitement, the spontaneous enthusiasm is as combustible as a fire among open containers of gasoline. Contagion is regarded as one of the hallmarks of true praise!

Another interesting reality of today's church is that praise has become one of its primary messages. I approach that observation with a bit of chagrin because I'm not sure that recent church start-ups are aware that the primary message of the church must always be centered in the salvific sacrifice of Jesus Christ as the savior of the world! When all is said and done, the role of the church remains that of bringing people into relationship with God through Jesus Christ! While praise is essential in maintaining a healthy relationship with God, it does not serve as God's agent for salvation. Simply stated, praise can best be accomplished within the experience of salvation, rather than salvation being accomplished within the experience of praise!

There are churches that emphasize praise as their primary message. Make no mistake about it, praise is an essential function of worship. However, I contend that "real praise" goes beyond the emotional, physical, and audible expressions of praise. Real praise requires living within God's purpose for which such creation was created. Often, the atmosphere of such "praise-heavy" churches is more akin to a pep rally than an assembly of learners eager to become more knowledgeable of God. Such churches are springing up in the most nontraditional venues. Nowadays one can often hear the sounds of worship flowing from meeting rooms and hallways of hotels and motels in many metropolitan cities where traditional church buildings have been replaced with temporary meeting rooms. Some such churches have even opted to gather in malls and shopping centers where once bustling stores have been converted into modern sanctuaries and worship centers. I have seen young pastors negotiate long-term leases for the use of funeral home chapels as the venue to host their church services. I was appalled to discover one such pastor who utilized a local tavern with liquor bottles and pictures of women in various stages of dress (or undress, depending on one's perspective) lining the walls, as his church—his Praise Center. Ironically, the most dominant word in the name of this church was PRAISE! In some of the most unlikely places, worshipers respond to the call of praise in these contemporary church services.

Those who exist on the outside of the church are at a loss to explain what this phenomenon really means. Commentators suggest that Christians have lost their minds, or they are on a fast track towards doing so. But the truth is that the act of praise has actively been part of the church since its biblical establishment at Jerusalem on the day of Pentecost. One can read in the Book of Acts, that in the upper room there was a sound of a rushing mighty wind that filled the whole house. The Bible continues that there appeared unto them cloven tongues like as of fire that set upon each of them! The emotional excitement of the day of Pentecost was so extensive that the crowd gathered in Jerusalem could hear those Christians speaking as if they were next to them. On that day, the activity of worship became the drawing card that resulted in the conversion of more than three thousand people.

But, of course, it was not just the New Testament church that reverberated in the emotional ecstasy of praise; the Old Testament psalmist often spoke of praise in an active tense. King David was often depicted as dancing before the Lord! His call for worship and praise echoes throughout the centuries; it can be heard clearly in the hearts of today's Christians in every continent upon the earth. Even beyond the Psalms, praise was as much a part of the children of Israel's odyssey in and out of Egypt as any other "God activity." Both major and minor prophets can often be seen and heard giving God praise. Worship was as much a part of the lives of godly men and women of biblical days as it must be in the lives of those who attempt to follow the teachings of Christ in today's church.

The question I wish to raise in this concluding lesson of this book is: Do we know what real praise is? And secondly, does our praise rise to the level of God's expectation of praise? How does God feel about our praise? Contemporary gospel singer Christopher Brinson released a song in 1997 that was echoed by church choirs and praise teams throughout the country. It rang in worship halls large and small: "What if God is unhappy with our praise?" Of all the questions raised by gospel music, this is perhaps one of the most relevant. It is because of that relevance, and many of the notions I have witnessed as I travel the country preaching and teaching about God's expectations of those who labor under the banner of the Lord's church, and especially those who labor as church leaders, that I have chosen to address the topic of praise in this manual. And while my voice is by no means the absolute voice on praise and worship, it is my prayer that this brief discussion of praise, and the church leader's responsibility to practice and understand praise, might be beneficial as our leaders evaluate their commitment towards "real praise" as a necessary ingredient in the church. Make no mistake about it, *"for praise is comely for the upright"* (Psa. 33:1).

I used the term "real praise" in both the title of this lesson and in the paragraph above in order to differentiate between praise, and what

I call "real praise." While the writer of the Psalms is considered the most prolific writer on the subject of praise, one such text in Psalm 150 suggests a closer look at how one interprets praise: *"Let every thing that hath breath Praise the Lord. Praise ye the Lord"* (Psa. 150:6).

When we evaluate all biblical suggestions surrounding praise, we must conclude that not everything that *"hath breath"* is capable of doing all of the things suggested by modern praise. However, everything that breathes can praise God. The context of this book does not allow me to expound deeply on the possible theory that I call *"God Praise!"* I am currently working on a book that I have titled, *"God Praise: A Biblical Look at How God Views Praise."* In the interest of closure for the moment, I will ponder that in order for everything that has breath to praise the Lord, then praise would have to be connected to purpose. What then is the purpose for which God made everything? We know that for everything there is a purpose. *"The Lord made everything for a purpose, even the wicked for an evil day"* (Prov. 16:4 CEB).

I suggest in my upcoming book that real praise can only be achieved as one's God-given purpose is being fulfilled. A tree praises God when it lives in the purpose for which God created it. How do the approximate 9,500 species of the dung beetle praise God? Dung beetles praise God as they consume poo throughout their life cycles. Dung beetles get their name from their diet of animal poo. Wherever there are herbivorous mammals leaving droppings, there are dung beetles making the most of it. *"Let every thing that hath breath Praise the Lord."* This text can be rendered: *"Let every thing that hath breath* [live in the purpose for which it was created] *Praise the Lord."* Psalms 145:10 confirms: *"All thy works shall praise thee, O Lord"* (Psa. 145:10); and can be rendered: *"All thy works shall* [fulfill the purpose for which they were created] *praise thee, O Lord."*

Church leaders, by virtue of their status of being chosen by God—saved by God, called by God, qualified by God—are thus, created by God. All thy works shall [fulfill the God-given purpose for which you were created] praise thee, O LORD.

Church leaders must practice "real praise"!

If You Enjoyed This Book, Will You Help Me Spread the Word?

There are several ways you can help me get the word out about the message of this book…

- Visit my website, and leave a review: 52principlesforchurchleaders.com

- Recommend the book to friends and fellow church leaders. Word of mouth is still the more effective form of advertising.

- Purchase additional copies to give away as gifts.

- Post a 5-Star review on Amazon, Goodreads and other places that come to mind.

- Write about the book on your Facebook, Twitter, Instagram, Google+, any social media sites you regularly use.

- Post a photo of yourself with the book on your social media.

- Ask bookstores if they carry the book. If not, they can easily order it through all major distributors.

- If you blog, consider referencing the book, or publishing an excerpt from the book with a link back to the website where you bought it.

- Do you know a podcaster, journalist or media personality who might be willing to interview me or write an article based on the book?

- Contact me by email at 52principlesbook@gmail.com.

www.ingramcontent.com/pod-product-compliance
Lightning Source LLC
Chambersburg PA
CBHW061609120626
46550CB00004B/1664